PUBLISHER'S NOTE

It is our belief that Robert Boldman has experienced a level of spiritual insight not often encountered in the contemporary West. His experiences have been confirmed subsequently by scriptures of the Eastern traditions. Because the author has spent several decades in intensive practice connected with various spiritual traditions, his book will be of particular interest to readers who have some familiarity with meditation or other forms of spiritual practice. Because the material covers several decades and is quite detailed, the author has limited his book primarily to aspects of his life experience that relate most directly to spiritual concerns.

The Alchemy of Love

A Pilgrimage of Sacred Discovery

Robert Boldman

for Loree,
wife and spiritual half

Copyright © 1997
by Robert Boldman

All rights reserved, including the right to reproduce this work in any form whatsoever, without permission in writing from the publisher, except for brief passages in connection with a review.

Cover design by Cisneros Design, Santa Fe, New Mexico
Cover photo by Loree Besch Boldman
Drawings © 1997 by Robert Boldman
Text composition by John Cole GRAPHIC DESIGNER, Santa Fe, New Mexico

For information write:

Heartsfire Books
500 N. Guadalupe St., Suite G-465, Santa Fe, NM 87501

If you are unable to order this book from your local bookseller, you may order directly from the publisher. Quantity discounts for organizations are available. Call (800) 988-5170, toll-free.

ISBN 1-889797-03-0

10 9 8 7 6 5 4 3 2 1

Printed on acid-free paper in Canada

Contents

Acknowledgments   ix
Introduction   xi

PART ONE   Into the Sea of Light

Chapter One 2
A Child on the Spiritual Path   At birth there was a nocturnal voice…

Chapter Two 16
Encounter with the Infinite   Whatever is asked God answers with light…

Chapter Three 23
Pursued by Death   …we must trust enough to plunge blindly…

Chapter Four 38
Awakening to the World   …pour with the rains, and sing God's praises…

Chapter Five 43
The Net of Kundalini   Our awareness thick with light, the Lion of Brahman on our breath…

Chapter Six 52
Choiceless Awareness:
The Fire of Bare Attention   Jesus' footprints are still on the Red Sea…

Chapter Seven 58
The Law of Suffering   The plain stone of attention is much more precious.

Chapter Eight 64
A Spiritual Wayfarer in the West   When the heart grows eyes we see nothing but riches.

Chapter Nine 69
The Mind in Emptiness   All the unimaginable worlds… beneath the petals of the heart.

CHAPTER TEN 76
  Enduring the Void   What we have lost
                               in silence will be reclaimed…

CHAPTER ELEVEN 82
  Riding the Current of Death   …death is the precious jewel;
                                  rebirth is the refiner's fire …

CHAPTER TWELVE 91
  Gift of the Goddess   … quicker than light she unfurls
                               each of a thousand petals.

PART TWO *The Ladder in the Heart*

CHAPTER THIRTEEN 98
  The Priest in the Garden   When the flower
                               of the heart is picked
                               it blows into the light.

CHAPTER FOURTEEN 108
  To Be Mad and Loving   When the mind is lush with fire
                               and slain with love…

CHAPTER FIFTEEN 119
  Becoming Visible to God   …Jesus and Shiva
                               dancing where there is no form…

CHAPTER SIXTEEN 127
  A Breath in God's Wind   …the sail of our spirits,
                               the ocean of blinding light.

CHAPTER SEVENTEEN 136
  The Legend of Father Thomas   …the tomb of his heart rolled open
                                  and love's brightness poured out…

PART THREE *A Shoulder to the Wheel*

CHAPTER EIGHTEEN 146
  The Tale Within the Tale   …among the waves
                               are many secrets…

Chapter Nineteen 154
The Death of Ego The roots of devotion must be burned…

Chapter Twenty 164
Shattering the Emptiness …washed from my heart, precious dreams just ornaments…

Chapter Twenty-One 169
Spiritual Rebirth …a single lotus flower transforms the darkness…

Chapter Twenty-Two 180
A Sacred Vocation Awakened by the pleading wind the Buddha is upon the plain…

Chapter Twenty-Three 192
Abandoning Truth and Merging with Love Open your arms wide and permit the Ganges to flow through…

Chapter Twenty-Four 198
At Rest in Awakening We should not march our spirits but usher them in singing…

Chapter Twenty-Five 205
Toward Simplicity: A Final Pilgrimage Love is my only song.

Afterword 213
The Practice of Inquiry The light that sees is the eternal light…

Notes 217
Glossary 218

*The ladder in the heart leads
to the summit of tantra,
to the heaven of Jesus,
to the abode of Shiva
to the bones of Nirvana,
to the sacred bond of love.*

Acknowledgments

I would mention first my spiritual guides, particularly the priest and sage under the name of Father Thomas, who is at the heart of this present work. I bow to Ramana Maharshi for taking birth on the plain of south India and to the many Tibetan masters who have been evicted from their homeland, bringing west with them a wisdom we are desperately in need of.

I would like to thank Oliver Beaudette for his warmth and encouragement and for patiently extracting the book from a novice author. I thank the inspiring figure of Claude Saks for leading the rest of us into the wilderness. I am indebted to my editor, Sara Held, for honing the text with her own spiritual wisdom.

It was an honor working with the entire press at Heartsfire Books, for theirs is a sacred journey that just happens to appear in printed form.

I would thank my mother and father first. And my wife last, for without her support and labors there would be no book. In between are those who walked the path with me, appearing in a host of disguises in the pages of this book. I am inexhaustibly indebted to each of them.

Introduction

My journey began as a child, my spiritual path beginning with first memory. The maze of spiritual experiences in childhood led me into the traditions of the East, through many states of meditative absorption and even miracles. But I was never rooted, never found what I was seeking. Along the way I was frequented with the cold bath of death experiences and wild plays of energy. These spiritual puzzles compounded until I met with a priest with an ancient message to deliver.

Father Thomas taught quite simply that the stream of love is ever pouring into and all around us, animating and dreaming us. Thus, he explained, to spontaneously and mindlessly love is to reclaim the message of Jesus. Yet he embraced many paths as the flowing wisdom of the Divine, even as Christianity remained most indelibly upon his heart.

For years I have studied the mystery that Father Thomas embodied and never have been able to satisfactorily explain most of what occurred between us. Playfully he both hid from me and surprised me, coaxing and tutoring me along the path of love. By turns I accepted and rejected the priest and kept the entire affair secret, preferring to return to my former meditation practices or worldly pursuits. It was years before I was able to submit to his wisdom.

Over the years I kept journals and once attempted to arrange them in a coherent form, but finally decided it was not a project worth pursuing. In that text, written in the middle of the 1980s, I merely noted Father Thomas in passing. But as I matured in spiritual matters I began to reexamine the affair of Father Thomas, and he reappeared to me in subtler forms to reassert himself and his message. It was made apparent then that Father Thomas had never been apart from me, that the alchemical flow he had initiated had guided me.

In the summer of 1995, at my wife's urging, I began recalling all that I could about this remarkable priest. The manuscript I originally drafted was simply about my meetings with Father Thomas. The project eventually grew into a text that included my life. This work became his work, a simple communication of a love that is both uncompromising and nameless. It is the fire of illumination for which I had always been searching.

Father Thomas's message is not about seeking God or piously approaching Him. He insists upon utter immersion in the Divine so that on earth a spiritual renaissance can be born. His path includes all that is sacred and all that can be expressed as love. Through him it was made apparent to me that all the masters and Buddhas were of the same nature and had been seated beneath the same boddhi tree as Father Thomas.

This book is not so much a personal history as a reflection of our shared spiritual nature. Within this text I reach out with the most direct realization that I am capable of summoning. I am not claiming to be a sage, but rather claiming that we are all entitled to Buddhahood, that we are all heir to spiritual wisdom.

My journey passed through most forms of spiritual worship and attainment. Such attainments are as inexhaustible as our thirst for them. Realization is a boundless transparency against which any experience can be held, even our own death. But no mere experience can cling to it or mark it; this is where the journey is ever leading.

The primordial wisdom of a realized being springs up spontaneously and can be expressed in a multitude of ways. With fierce sermons John the Baptist demanded that we repent. Jesus walked the shore of an ancient sea, spinning sweet parables. There have been sages who have gushed with miracles and sages who have held such displays in utter contempt. Spiritual figures have been poets, have sung and danced ecstatically; sages have engaged in philosophical debate and held vows of silence. Krishna had a thousand lovers and Buddha looked upon lovers as spiritual poison. There have been sages serene and composed and sages improper and humorous. Sages have hidden quietly away in caves and sages have shouted and ranted in attempts to trick the mind. Jesus rejoiced in a feast as a respite from his harsh wanderings, yet in his name saints have refused all sustenance except for a daily Eucharist. The Divine nature is swifter than the mind and therefore cannot be grasped or explained. We must accept that. There is no undamaged thread through all the sages of our past except that of love, the gentle touch of Buddhahood and the thunderous message of the saints.

PART ONE

Into the Sea of Light

Chapter One

A Child on the Spiritual Path

*At birth there was a
nocturnal voice,
wet from the sea;
the lamp of the spirit
held up for the senses.*

I was born at the sun's apex in the middle of the century, on June 22, 1950. According to my mother I was a "shrunken, ugly old man, with long, stiff legs." A pitiable, dispiriting sight as a firstborn, with skin such a deep umber that it appeared I had been scorched from exposure to the sun. Breaths were held back from rejoicing and there were murmurs among my aunts, to which my mother responded with a glare. For his part, my father, ever prone to flushing the humor out of a situation, commented that he was just relieved that I looked like him, only older.

That was to prove a hard winter, for I was sick many nights, often requiring medicines that my father had to fetch by hiking to the drug store, even when the blizzard of 1950 raged. If he had not been pulled from a snow drift one night by a passerby, he might well have frozen to death.

I grew up in a ramshackle area bordering Wright Patterson Air Force Base just outside of rural Fairborn, Ohio. Wright Patterson was then home of the SAC bombers and the most crucial target for the Russians, a distinction of which we were reminded with each jet that stormed over our house, shattering windows and upsetting cups.

During the heat of World War II, Air Force dependents, most from the backwoods it seemed, had been provided marginally habitable apartments that stretched in a stagnant march across bare fields not yet cemented into hangars and air strips. It was in this exodus from home towns that my mother was uprooted from the bayous of northern Louisiana, both of her brothers having enlisted and her sister having married a soldier. According to a portrait of her surviving that era, my mother was jauntily pretty and defiant. I look at her as an apparition from a prenatal dream, arriving upon a hard road from the rural south without a father. She was raised upon miles of unmarked swamp, her task to work in the fields about their tin-roofed shack. Sweet in repose, my mother was formidable when aroused—her heart was the resonance of our home. I grew up in seamless kinship with her.

Her mother, worn by years of hardship, was an almost ghost-like presence. She raised four children along a harsh swamp without a husband to depend upon—he had died suddenly when she was pregnant with my mother. Nanny's attributes and dreams, thereafter, were sublimated to raising her brood. Crude and untalkative, she was a product of the poor regions of the bayou, dipping snuff and wearing dresses with no labels from thrift shops. But she was also undeniably resourceful and determined, forging a path for her children.

My mother's grandmother was a seer, or what would now be referred to as a healer and channeler. A pagan among Christians, she supposedly had a talent for reeling in spirits, enabling her to perform minor wonders and minister to the sick. According to town legend, she wandered along its roads "with the spirit upon her," seeing the unseen, mumbling into the ineffable. But my mother's warmest regard was reserved for her great-grandmother, a French refugee from the purges in the late 1800s who never mastered English but spoke in gestures, gestures that my mother repeated to me.

My father was raised in Fairborn, Ohio, moving from house to house within sight of Wright Patterson Air Force Base. In 1932 he was famous, for just a week. The tale, headlined in newspapers throughout the world, was about a boy and his trusted dog. My father was then just four and was resting on the porch behind their house when he was attracted into the yard. As he ambled for the garden, the family dog, a usually pleasant Doberman by the name of Blackie, leaped upon him, sending him tumbling. Harshly scolded by my father's parents, Blackie retreated, but when my father again approached the garden, Blackie repeated his performance, for which he was whipped. Stubbornly, my father aimed again for the garden and Blackie rushed out from under the porch and bounded over him and onto a rattlesnake sunning itself on the path to the garden. Blackie ripped apart the snake and in turn received a number of bites, lying near death for almost a week as the story went out on the wires. Updates on Blackie's condition were even tacked onto newsreel footage. The dogs Blackie sired, for years afterward, fetched a steep price. And for years my grandfather held onto the newspaper clippings, proof of the dog's worth. Twenty years later my father was living less than a mile from where this happened.

Though a laborer by trade and sent off to work when he was just twelve, my father was famous in his haunts for jitterbugging to the Big Bands. From the photographs, my parents should have stormed the dance halls, both wonderfully made up for a night out, the pair of them just waking up from their poor, rural upbringings. In each print they are almost rushing past the lens, heedless in their pursuit of a buoyant joy they had never found except as a couple. When fixed upon with a camera, my father just leaned on his innate grace, casually looking away from the lens.

My father lived across the road from the Air Force housing in the slums, most of whose folks were drawn north from the hills of Kentucky in search of an honest trade. Arranged in clans that packed into cramped inhospitable shacks, a number of these reckless folks harbored pistols beneath their shirts and engaged in sacred games of poker each night. In winter they huddled about coal burners that never warmed their porous rooms, and once it was summer they became rooted to porches that pitched like ships' decks.

A coal miner in West Virginia since he was eight, as a young man my grandfather had been arrested for murder and sentenced to trucking munitions among the trenches of World War I. Upon his return stateside, he was rewarded with a post as a trucker on the base. Transporting uranium west during World War II, he was eventually stricken with radiation sickness, for the minerals were stored in plain crates and it was his habit to nap at night in the rear of the truck.

Although it may have not seemed like much, my grandfather's plank and tarpaper house with a mud cellar was prized, for it had plumbing and heat. This was what I was born to, and it was among those rooms that mind and memory explicitly began.

Memory began when I was floundering in diapers, attempting to straddle my frail legs and walk, and I was raw from pitching over on the kitchen floor. Among those present was a heartily amused aunt and a pair of cousins nearly my age. We were perched on the brink of the kitchen, the floor into the next room sloping away, when at a precise instant I acquired a self—was suddenly alone within myself. Until then I had just been swept along, abundantly nourished and pampered, mindlessly abiding. With the harmless jeering of my aunt, a motion in me had been signaled to and I had been jostled out of the present, taking up residence in a self. Only then, by my reckoning, was I delivered to the world.

Prior to this moment, the present was just inexhaustibly flowing into itself in its eternal, almost motionless passage. This is the most indestructible memory I carry with me, for the enterprise of becoming had just been initiated: wordlessly I had been translated from the realm of being to becoming—I both possessed and was possessed by a self.

Crippled and deranged from radiation poisoning, my paternal grandfather steered about our house in a wheelchair and I fled in his wake. My grandmother supported him by working in the print shop on the base, for in an orphanage she had acquired a proper tutoring in English. Aunt Mary slept in the rear bedroom. Except in the months of mid-winter, my grandmother slept on the screened-in porch. Because I slept on the couch in the parlor just inside the porch, my grandmother's presence there seemed to secure my sleep. My makeshift bed was an island of warmth next to the grate for the coal furnace.

On that same couch I was granted an audience with the Virgin. I was no more than two and recall that it was in winter because the coal grate was furiously glowing. Graced with a jewel-like splendor, the Virgin poured over me tenderly, as though I were being submitted to her for a scrupulous blessing. Although my grandmother had been baptized and raised in Saint Luke's orphanage, I had not met with the icon of the Virgin. So I assumed that it was an angel, presuming this until, at almost six years old, I encountered her in a niche of a church sanctum.

I never shared this tale, for it seemed to be a secret in need of protecting. She returned when I was ailing or dispirited, the illumined figure a vehicle of blessing. Oddly, once I named the image the visitations ceased. In retrospect it seems she vanished because an emerging self would not permit an inner beloved to manifest. By naming her I had resigned her to a residence from which I related to her as just imaginary.

As the apparition of the Goddess faded I became obsessed with the act of *witnessing*. Being compelled to look and examine is what I recall most from boyhood. There was an almost primal need to look, to gather with my eyes, although my mind remained patiently quiet, clean of all that I gathered. There was much to be the witness of in Wright View Heights. There were thugs and whores on the dim roads; the night was haunted. On the slope beneath our house, among the trailers between the junk yard and the bar, lived twin boys with numerous crippling birth defects who had never been to a doctor. I befriended them, though I preferred solitude in which unimpeded "seeing" could be engaged. The task of witnessing became so innate, my senses so sharpened on the natural rhythms about me, that most grownups found me infuriatingly mute and complacent. In the first grade I was repeatedly hazed and slapped by a teacher who became enraged when I refused to harness my mind to her projects. The more she rampaged, the more I withdrew into mute witnessing, never expressing even a mild protest. When she scolded me I examined her with care, but I rejected the entire affair of cramming the mind with facts, for such a practice hampered the ritual of seeing I had adopted. At a teacher's request in the second or third grade, I was examined for signs of being unreachably disturbed or impaired, but returned with a note pronouncing me fit.

The seasons arced over our house and most days I was holed up in the field just to the east of our property, engaged in my sacred vigil. I hunched over nature, relentlessly regarding its motion, and when my gaze was penetrating enough the things of nature seemed to glow, providing enough light to wake even a stone from its slumber. The more I looked at a thing, the more its inherent light was revealed to me. It was as though my labors had opened a pair of more penetrating eyes that allowed me to see into the soul of an object.

This was my craft of "seeing," an art which mesmerized me. All of nature was an upsurge of tides and cadences of light. When my concentration was most intense, the scene before me was engulfed in an almost blinding radiance. The nature of my "seeing" was just a purposeless joy. To me, then, the entire earth was wonderfully animate, returning breath to me as I hovered upon its waking back. I never uprooted a stone without pursuing a home for it, without calming it and cradling it against me. My self was just a pure seeing enamored with light.

All that I met with ebbed into light, each chapter of the day dedicated to meeting with the ghosts that inhabited the entire world, that pulsed even within the mice nesting in our garage—even a worm had a spiritual inheritance and a task to perform in this world. Of this I was convinced. And so I was mandated to care for the field and robbed our almost bare kitchen for morsels; I mended nests and quilted stones into a path. My mind rested in a quiet which I refused to harness to the mere act of recording. In class I was considered a daydreamer, intractably vacant. I looked upon even the most practical memorization as an affront and had to be reminded of my room number afresh many days. My inner precincts were too sacred to me to be shackled to mere ideas. I much preferred my mind to be relaxed, permitted merely to roam or gaze into unthinkable depths.

Eventually we moved to a cinder block house nearby, just two houses from my grandmother's; my aunt and grandmother remained approachably near. I roomed in the attic along with my mother's manual sewing machine, her mannequin, and stacks of wax patterns. Here my mother worked at her sewing, which she had taken in since childhood. But the attic was my province each evening except when Nanny, my grandmother from Louisiana, visited and shared my quarters. She was an insatiable reader, and when she bedded with me I was treated to a children's book and then the rustling of pages from her western novels lulling me to sleep.

My mother was at the hub of my world, her quaint adages about hope and God and her burning pride providing me with a sanctuary when we were most harshly poor. She worked to instill me with God, without expecting me to conform. She exposed me to numerous beliefs. She was herself prone to a belief in reincarnation. She accepted my peculiarities without trying to alter me or expecting me to retrace her path. She projected herself onto me, but only the best of herself.

As his father, my father was composed of bedrock. He was generous and amiable, his inexhaustible wit ever racing. He worked then at unskilled labor, reporting to work at sunrise. As were my Aunt Mary and my father's mother, we were poor; but I was never wounded by neglect or want.

When I was six, I almost drowned, an event which had deep repercussions. My parents were fond of cane pole fishing in the tideless, almost unflowing murk of a nearby river. There were not many fish about; it was more of a relaxation done in peaceful accord with a river. I adored this ritual, especially when it was carried out at night: the unseen splashes of their casts, the aura of the lantern beneath the glittering night—even the trips to forage for bait prior to the expedition.

On the night fixed in memory, they were fishing the dark swirl by the glow of a kerosene lantern, its flame hissing and cremating moths. My father was migrating upstream, intent on seeking carp beneath the bridge spanning the state route. Almost as quickly as he vanished from the lantern's glow, I was hobbling in pursuit. Plummeting into the river is not a memory I am able to conjure, nor can I be reminded of inhaling the dank water. My memory begins with just sinking, without a hint of resisting, for I was imagining being sucked into the river—much of it was pleasant. As I plunged deeper I grew lighter until it dawned upon me that I was no longer inside a body and just then began rising from the murkiness. And then I was rejoicing, for in a rush I was again "in myself," and so rose without even sparing a glance for the river, surging up and up, racing toward a home that had been all but erased from my mind but which I was suddenly desperately seeking. A wind had swept into me and I was rising on it. Then I was within a whirling tunnel formed of this unseen wind. There were no words in mind; I was just rejoicing and returning home. The longing was almost unbearable as the light I recognized from my "seeing" dawned before me. And then I was yanked from the river to the bank, gasping for breath in my father's arms. And at that precise instant I was aware that I was capable of again rushing away; it was the love I read in my father's eyes that returned me to the world.

I was altered by the experience. An ancient past had been returned to me and the world I was in suddenly seemed a horror to be endured. I had an overwhelming feeling that I had made the decision to be born and that I was part of an experiment, that I was being watched. But the experiment was of my design and depended entirely upon my capabilities. Even as a child of six I held onto these ideas as indisputable. The horror of this world and its unstemmed pains was ever in mind; and I began to look upon birth here as a mistake, as a horrendous mistake that needed to be amended. There seemed no hope, no redemption for this world—I was, I presumed, a spirit in exile. I ranted; I wept. There was much then I was able to recall about my previous life, the details of which ebbed away as I grew up.

I regretted later I had not drowned. The longer I was in this body the more it seemed a prison; this world was bleak and painful compared to the majesty of the world I had left behind. Yet I was immature and confused, unable to understand what was expected of me.

I began having dreams that were journeys leading to worlds of light and happiness. Although these worlds were not the home I longed for, they seemed near to it. So I began looking for a passage from the outer dream into the "inner dream" in which such worlds could be found. Dreams appeared to my immature mind as islands in a dark space, and beneath these islands were worlds of boons and happiness. When paradise was later bantered about in church, it was these worlds to which my mind referred.

I began searching for a passage similar to the one I experienced when I almost drowned. By day I scoured the untended fields and pastures near our house, searching for a picture to dream—a picture with a passage by which I could enter the inner worlds. When I found what looked like a passageway, such as the gopher burrows in my field or the lightning-struck tree along the road or the whirlpool in the stream in the cow pasture, I would hunch over them and memorize them, apparently already aware that I forged the day's events into a dream language at night.

My parents forbade my wanderings, but I was not harshly punished. According to my mother's recollections I just kept vanishing, no matter what reproof descended upon me. My practice of seeing light in nature was permanently set aside, replaced with a quest across woods and fields. I was intent upon finding a passage that would lead me to my inner home; the hidden light was no longer of consequence to me.

What I usually latched onto as the subject of my dreams was the storage hatch on the landing upstairs. I dreamed most often about my room with its slanted ceiling and my shelf of children's books beside the bed. When I was able to maintain my composure and walk across the dream to the hatch, I was able to step across into a magnificent kingdom, although in these realms I flitted about like a phantom and only rarely was I noticed by the people inhabiting these kingdoms. So I gradually adopted the view that I was a resident of neither this world nor that. I grew perplexed and incapable, prone to mishaps. The people in my waking world were strange to me, their habits nonsensical. The world was heartless, my interior all that I was in accord with.

Sketching became my consuming task. At first I labored over what appeared as random corridors, which was an attempt to map out my nightly transports. I reimagined those sojourns as mazes on a page. Then I began drawing courses I might take in future dreams. When I had no paper I sketched my mazes in the dirt. I could not put what was happening to me in words so I drew, the only way to transfer the secrets of that world into this one. Each page I drew grew more ornate, the mazes more petaled, as my fingers pored over their sacred content, holding the invisible up to light. When Nanny told me the story of Jacob's ladder as a way of climbing to heaven I spent days and nights imagining what it might look like and putting it on paper. From the way she described it, this ladder to heaven was exactly the passage for which I had been searching.

Gradually it was decided that my dreaminess in class indicated a creative impulse and I was called upon to paint and draw, which I credibly managed. And I was taken into the fold; I had a talent for art—I was not just passive and dreamy. I had a purpose. Teachers who had once heaped scorn upon me were marking a path that would permit me a smooth passage. But I received no solace from this change, for I had not been seeking to impress, but to make an imprint of a spiritual wilderness. Perhaps I was even attempting to make a usable map. I was no more than eight when it began, but these inner assumptions were about to be shattered.

The most remarkable of these childhood events began with the Pentecostal church on the sloping road along the field by my house. Tacked on the side of a hill and presiding over the neighborhood's weed-choked baseball diamond was a plain white clapboard church without sign or emblem. Each evening at about dusk it overflowed with song and praise, the singing so sweet, the praise so wild that it was as though angels and devils were holding hands and shouting down heaven. I found the many voices of the church enrapturing, so perfectly met from the field at the base of the slope.

Reaching the church from our house was just a matter of slipping through an untended field, across a neighboring yard and onto the baseball field. Often after supper, when my parents assumed I was playing in the back yard, I slipped toward the church just at dusk in the rhythmic patterns of fading light. Dusk was magical—though not as magical as what I witnessed at the church. Mere laborers and farmers with plain, dull-looking wives and children, once inside the church and out of my sight, were utterly transformed by song and dance into strange voices, shouts, weeping, as though once inside they were able to dream aloud. Or were wrapped up in God.

My part in the affair was to stretch out among the weeds, overjoyed with the strange praise, while the stars grew above me. I was at peace, accepting what was ahead of me, for it seemed I had uncovered an important secret embedded in normal, waking life. Each night waves of energy radiated from the church, energy that saturated both me and the night air. On occasion I was roused to sway and dance, pretending that I was among the worshipers. It was my magic and my secret.

On a particular evening, though, a strange tremor began. It was extremely unpleasant and entered me from deep in the earth, a rushing, harsh energy seeking a point far above where I stood. I tumbled to the raw-smelling earth, where I remained, filled with

a quiet light that seemed to be the residue of the experience. When I woke from my trance, the church was quiet and dark, yards and houses in shadow. When I attempted to stand, my body did not work properly; my legs were hobbled and stiff.

But the process had just begun. I soon became more disjointed and confused, lights appearing in my mind then quickly fluttering away, the sense of my body rapidly expanding and contracting. At night I sleeplessly floated on an unseen tide of light. Unlike my previous encounters in nature, this light was harsh and menacing. I was helpless in the grasp of these energies. But what worried me was not what would happen to me, but what my parents would think if I were exposed. Ever since I started school it had grown increasingly apparent I was not like the rest of the children, that I was not normal. And I was prepared to endure whatever was necessary in order that my parents never discover this.

My legs were particularly affected by the experience, and as the days passed they grew weaker. I was partially lame, a fact which I managed to hide, remaining in my room with my books each night, not so unusual, and remaining in my seat during lunch and recess, behavior which was not even noticed by my teachers. I would usually wait until all the children had run for the bus and then hobble in their wake, but on a particular day I found I could not stand and so just remained in my seat. If a teacher had not returned for her papers to be graded I may have remained until my parents searched. I wept and confessed that I was not capable of walking, although I did not divulge then or ever the reason. I was seen by a doctor who, finding no tangible problem, assumed that it was a plea for help. Gradually my legs returned to full strength, but the entire affair was a reminder to avoid the Pentecostal church, which my parents had not approved of to begin with.

Although I suspected what had happened to me was a punishment, perhaps even from God, a process of awakened energies had begun that would remain with me, shaping and prodding me along, the explanation not to be searched out for two decades more and the point of it all to elude me for even longer. But these energies did push me out of my quiet repose. I temporarily left my dream world behind, for I found that in order to compensate for these experiences I needed to be physical. So I began running along the road to our house until I was winded, engaging in games at recess, perpetually in motion until my physical nature was wrapped snugly about me.

I was, I knew, approaching what was respected and normal. By the time I was twelve I looked back on my spiritual past as a defect—for I had no method of interpreting my experiences. They were oddities, even signs of madness. So I worked against them, working to be accepted. I rejected God. My mother still made a point of taking me on her expeditions to a host of churches, but I had no sympathy for any of it except the paragons of Catholic saints, and those solely because I knew that my paternal grandmother loved them. A sweet woman with a devout heart even though she never attended mass, she died when I was away from home at summer camp at twelve, marking the ending of all that belonged to the precious imaginings of childhood. I kept her picture in my dresser for months, but finally decided to pack even this away, for I had to be done with illusions.

The rampant energies did not vanish entirely until I reached puberty, but the energies that once seemed very spiritual now seemed part of ordinary physical processes. I continued to exercise, to jog and swim, but remained most dedicated to painting and sketch work—for which I was praised and amply rewarded. And this was to remain my identity until a most remarkable event shook me out of it in college.

Chapter Two

Encounter with the Infinite

> *Whatever is asked*
> *God answers with light;*
> *whatever is expected*
> *death is at the door.*
> *This is my sutra and tantra.*

In 1969 I was a student in Fine Arts at Wright State University, schooling which I funded with a job at a small children's hospital in Dayton, Ohio. Although I initially viewed this work as an unpleasant necessity, I have ever since moved among jobs in hospitals, my few skills as a painter gradually abandoned. I was hired as night orderly, with a host of ill-defined, ever-changing tasks.

I was stationed each night in the emergency room, unlocking the doors if a patient arrived, paging a nurse from the floor, and then waking the doctor. I wrote out the charts, determined the need of the patient, assisted the doctors and nurses when called upon, cleaned, and guarded the single door into the hospital. Few patients rang in at night and I usually pored over books or chess problems, my chessboard and tournament pieces on the counter. I learned about affairs in Europe, Asia, Africa, of their traditions and religions, from the number of foreign physicians who staffed the emergency room when the children's hospital was young. There was no one else for them to speak to, the nurses being occupied with patients in both the wards and the emergency room.

Late that summer, the hospital cared for a child who was wracked with leukemia, which steadily consumed her until her heart was finally stilled. The news of her death on a particular night in August came as relief, for she had been robbed of all but a dumb witnessing as she shrank upon her bones, the bed surrounding and engulfing her. I helped the nurse draw the shroud about her, binding her hands and tagging her feet before we transported her to the morgue. A sheet covered her as we moved through back halls and down service elevators.

Even if it is expected, even longed for, the death of a child is never fully appreciated until it finally happens. Death is ever new, and I found the death of this child numbing. As I pushed the cart through the halls in the basement toward the morgue, it seemed that life was so thin that wherever I turned I could see death through it. I was transfixed with her death; her death had become my death, which would be the death of us all. I had no faith in surviving death, even considered annihilation a possible blessing. What I witnessed of the child's death I fully believed—that the child had been consumed by a hunger that exceeded hers: that of the cancer. What was her and hers was not perpetual. When I returned to the desk I wrote a rambling poem and the remainder of the night just stared, all thought eluding me.

I was acquainted with death. As a child I had seen a man being hauled out of a car after hooking up his exhaust to kill himself. But in the case of the child I shared her death; her death was transposed upon me—for it was apparent without even thinking on the subject that I was destined to become her; we were joined.

As the week wore on I did not recover from the ordeal. I remained in bed, not reporting to classes or work. I was preparing to make a leap, for if I were to be annihilated it seemed as though I might as well get on with it. I had looked into my mind, had dredged up as much of my past as I could, and had found no excuse for persisting. There was no direction that did not lead to death and vanishing, so if I were destined to be subtracted then I much preferred to choose the path than to have it randomly chosen for me—the routines nature depended upon were much too harsh.

That night, with this decision looming before me, I sought out Elaine. We had shared much. At seventeen, she had run away from an abusing home. I had joined her in a small apartment in a squalid part of town; eventually we were destitute and taken in by my family. Just as my family had housed needy children all through my childhood, they accepted Elaine. Eventually she found a new apartment, which because of working nights I seldom shared.

That night we had dinner and went off to bed. I had intended to explain to her, for I desperately wanted to communicate, but I just could not speak. I had been robbed of all will. It was as though I had become so fragile that just walking across a room jostled me painfully. Without preamble, I went to her bed and stretched out on my back, sinking into the quiet. Elaine put out the lights and settled in beside me on her back, never inquiring—though it was apparent that I was strangely afflicted. The window was half open and the night was wandering about outside, thick with wind and clouds. I found a patch of her skin and rested my hand there, as though at anchor in the dark. Quickly I relaxed and even grew calm, dropping off into a tranquil quiet so removed from my senses that it seemed my body was vanishing out from under me; and I was so relaxed that I would not have minded.

Oddly, I began reciting a poem, the poem I composed the night I had put the corpse of the young child in the morgue freezer, in a voice that did not seem to belong to me; it was as though I were hearing a second person from a distance, mumbling thoughts which I had once thought.

The poem warmed me and out of the warmth emerged a

pleasant shuddering—a vibration. The vibration swept over me, tuning my entire body even down to the cells, heating up every structure, until it seemed I was on the verge of becoming one of those grotesque victims of spontaneous combustion. I was incapable of responding, could not even ponder what was happening. Just when it seemed that the body could bear no more, that I would burst into flame, I was thrown from my body.

I was aware of moving at an astounding speed, exceeding, I was sure, all motion thought possible, even that of light, as though this too were a burden to be cast off. Although my usual commenting mind was not present and there was no report from the senses, there was intuition—intuition that did not require the mind's imprint. I possessed no body, no form, but was a formless awareness speeding across an ineffable space.

What I sensed was that I was approaching infinity, or God; and as this was transpiring I was absorbed in a bliss against which all mere pleasure paled. This bliss was both a raw force, ripping me apart, and a current leading into God. Such exhilaration cannot be described, for it was apparent that the physical body dampens the mind. And it is not until we are free of its constraint that we can appreciate the wondrous nature of mind. A thought did occur to me then: *I never want to be alive again.*

What I was experiencing was not actually an ascent; once out of body I did not move in a particular direction. I was being undone, changed, moved into God, of that I was convinced. I wanted never to return to my body, to endure muddied senses and the body's numberless boundaries. The continuum of my life had been shed and I was racing and plummeting home. As I was approaching God, a splendid radiance, I thought of my mother, of a thing she had told me when I was a small child. She had said there was no worse fate for a mother than to outlive one of her children. With this, the experience was finished and I was thrown back into bed.

Energy hammered the inside of my skull, my senses returning to me from a great distance. My body moved as though not properly jointed. I was aroused, my skin flushed, my heart pounding furiously. I wanted to love and be loved; I wanted to seize Elaine. The energy of death had become a fountain of passion. I wanted to love her both richly and passionately, I wanted to embrace all and be embraced by all. This is what I had returned from God with. But it would be years before I appreciated what had happened and the link between sex and the energies I had unleashed.

I rose from the bed and found Elaine cringing against the wall, trembling all over as I approached. "What kind of man are you?" she asked in a whisper. I held her and when she was calm I found, without my prompting, that she had endured the same experience—we had shared this same glimpse of infinity. She explained that as she lay beside me the hand resting upon her stomach had begun to tingle and heat up. Whatever it was entered her and she began to vibrate, suddenly pulled out of her body. From there her experience was identical to mine, though she interpreted it more as a mingling of souls in God. I had not been aware of a "soul" apart from mine. We would repeatedly discuss and reexamine this strange experience.

We searched out explanations—discovered that we both had been profoundly affected. As a result, Elaine began channeling, which was deeply disturbing to her Christian roots and previously unfamiliar to both of us. For my part, I was filled with a spiritual appetite that was almost unbearably consuming. I imagined mountain retreats in India as well as images of saffron-robed monks in deep meditation. All the normal trappings of daily life that were once so alluring to me held no appeal. I longed to be a renunciate and wander without possessions, to belong only to God. Meats I once craved were suddenly unpalatable, and I resolved to be celibate.

But what I had assumed was lasting illumination gradually ebbed. Although my spiritual ardor continued to burn, it had been made apparent that the road ahead would be harder than first expected. The experience of God into which I had so easily catapulted would have to be approached again and arduously won. There was no setting aside what had happened. It had occurred and had been confirmed independently; there was no avoiding the matter and no excuse not to pursue it with all that I managed to conjure from within. Yet it was daunting; much was required and there was not much to sustain me as I searched, and I was not versed in the subject of spirituality. But this event marked a course in which I would exhaustively begin studying the world's spiritual paths, although there were meager resources at this juncture, mostly paperbacks on psychic phenomena and a few translations from the spiritual explorers of the early twentieth and late nineteenth centuries.

Once I was considered a promising artist and painter, but I soon found that the figure studies in which we were ever engaged held no appeal. There was a fierce urge in me to write. Seated on the edge of my bed in the basement of my parents' house, I furiously composed poems night after night, the need for sleep seldom arising.

Most importantly, I expected that I had been set upon the path of being a monk. I attended mass, which was like a secret wedding. And I imagined that I required no more sustenance than communion. When I sought counsel with a Franciscan monk, however, I found their routine quite numbing. It seemed they were endlessly engaged in mere ritual, a prescribed dance with a purpose I could not fathom.

I happened across the essays of D.T. Suzuki, the tiny Japanese sage who delivered Zen Buddhism to the West almost single-handedly. His rambling non-sayings upon the subject of enlightenment were profoundly intriguing to me. I imagined myself as just such a monk, shorn and wearing the ink-blot robes representing Zen's rich past. Since childhood, I had assumed that I would become a painter, that I would relocate to the East Coast and work at building a reputation. But that was past. I was looking to dedicate what I was to God, even the poetry I composed each night.

Anxious to share my experience, I was stunned when I was not only rejected but held up to scorn. I had been working a couple of evenings a week at a bookshop and had respected the owner—but when I related to him the tale of my death experience he accused me of being on drugs. I was baffled by his response and even more baffled when I found he was making the charges to my friends, all of whom frequented the shop. Rumors had it, within a couple of weeks, that I was drugged, deluded, raving about God. Perhaps he even convinced Elaine that she had been drugged, for soon she moved out of her apartment into his. Making no pretense, I explained what had happened among friends, but found that I was goaded, argued with and against, until the reports were amended and I was looked upon as deranged. The monk with whom I had been meeting suggested that I keep mum on the subject, even hinting that I had been possessed. Even close friends who did not immediately condemn the story were soon perplexed by my radical change in the wake of my death experience, for I was neither indulging in their pleasures nor interested in art. I even wrote poetry just as a form of praise, not to polish it into an art form. I was suddenly boring and quietly reserved. I had been singled out by my experience. A break had been made that could never be mended.

Chapter Three

Pursued by Death

*It is the spirit
not the body that needs
to be resurrected.
But we must trust
enough to plunge blindly
into a sea of light.*

I had not heard the term "near-death experience." Perhaps it had not even been coined in 1970, but as the months passed I was convinced I had died and returned. The body had remained behind on the bed, a hull without spirit, and I had been drawn out, or more accurately sped up, approaching the vibration in which God is met. Wordlessly the experience had communicated this to me.

I had no contact with a spiritual culture, no oral map upon which to depend, so I went forward, thinking over the course of many months that I had stepped out of the experience, that it was relegated to the past. Yet its current remained with me, for I was compelled to write, poetry just pouring out of me. Judging these poems was not significant for me—the need was to discharge the energies. In retrospect, it was plain that the map of transformation I was in need of had appeared and was subtly inhabiting my body, although its fullness was not readily apparent except as raw energies and images demanding to be translated into words. For me, then, the poems slowly created the guiding map which I had been ignoring.

I met Kathy working as a clerk at Children's Hospital. I immediately was attracted to her but she was engaged, and anyway I summed her up as more than I deserved. She was quiet, kind, and extremely bright and attended the same university on scholarship. Adept with languages, she carried books that tended to have indecipherable titles. Kathy was a year ahead of me in college and to make matters worse her fiancé was wealthy. But I began a campaign to win her, which succeeded, and on New Year's Eve of 1970 we were engaged.

I had normal hopes, as normal as any fine arts student is capable of, and though my nerves seemed to burn with spiritual energies I just accepted them as an aspect of my person, a creative sign of a poet—I even began to conform to an image of a poet I had both conjured up and gleaned from my readings. And at this point I failed to link the energies to my recent "death" experience.

At the time of my engagement to Kathy, I retained a single friend from the past—Rick. His parents had met during World War II in Europe, his father a tank commander and his mother a nurse. When Kathy and I married he practically moved in, repairing the house, building furniture, running errands. He found my experiences intriguing. He had once had a near-death experience, when he was struck by the rigging of a sail and tumbled unconscious into a lake. As he was limp in the water, his awareness rose and remained suspended above the scene as he was rescued. Perhaps as a result of this experience, he expressed a belief in reincarnation. Rick and I were to remain close for over a decade, until he enlisted in the army— for we had argued repeatedly upon the subject of the Vietnam War, which he seemed determined to become a part of. Kathy accepted my peculiarities and Rick's and my inseparability without a complaint.

The summer of our engagement, I had a second death experience, which made me reconsider engaging in spiritual practice. We were at my parents' house and it was late, so Kathy set-

tled in for the night on the upstairs couch. I went to my room in the basement. Preparing for bed, I was overwhelmed with a sense of not belonging in the room, as though I were intruding upon a person with whom I was not familiar. When I stretched out, I was seized by an overwhelming force, my body pinned against the sheets.

I was transported from my room and I found myself hiking on a plain, hills ahead white with heat. Yet I was not taken aback by this abrupt shift, for I had become the man hiking across a scorching plain. I had not just entered his form, but had wholly become that person. All that concerned me was a harsh desert wind opposing my steps and a flaming sun so intense that rushing clouds only faintly dimmed it. A man I was familiar with marched with me, his pace lagging just a step off mine. I made no reckoning except that we were upon an errand that led past the looming hills. Our crisp, pale robes glared back at the sun; the scene was rich, remarkably intense.

The earth trembled, and before us a band of riders arced into sight, their horses appearing beneath them as they crested a hill. There was no hiding and in any attempt to flee we would be quickly outstripped by the horses. So I came to a halt, my labored breath marking time as I watched the armored troop approach. When my companion spun and ran, a mounted soldier split from the rest and pursued him. Other riders were almost upon me and a spear was launched. I lunged forward, grasping the lance that impaled me. And in the next instant I was looking on the scene from the air as a soldier dismounted and examined his work.

The force that had pinned me to my bed seized me again, transporting me, helpless, away from the scene and into what appeared to be a long, dim passageway. I was plunging down halls, seeing portraits on walls, figures in rooms, which melted as the force quickened. All shape blurred—I was awash in raw emotion and mindless terror. All that remained was a sense of dying, against which I railed futilely, for this force was relentless. This was just death: there was no illumination, no passage, just a human mind being ripped apart by wild energies as though it were of no consequence. I wanted to scream, for I just then sensed that I might be dreaming. And perhaps if I screamed I would awaken. I thought I screamed, but the house and its occupants were quiet when I found myself back in bed, staring intently at the ceiling. I found Kathy and she held me, but even then I realized I could not be protected from whatever was happening to me.

Just as I suspected, I was not to elude this shadow that seemed to be upon me. Late that summer there was yet another encounter. I had just lain down when I began having a conscious dream. The images were more crisp and real than the images in my waking life, but as free as a pinwheel; I worked and worked, arranging them like a puzzle. I had never been the recipient of such a lucid dream. It was not until I was utterly distracted that I noticed the familiar force tugging at me, like an undertow. I attempted to remain calm, detached, for I had learned from previous experience that struggling only intensified its grasp.

I was in motion through numerous worlds, each world flourishing and unique in its aspects, and each of which I saw as a possible existence. When I did not resist this current I was caught up in, it appeared quite different. I was not being torn apart; I was being purified and remade by the energies that were harbored within this singular motion. What I was encountering was death not as an annihilation, but as a process in which I was being transformed.

I passed into realms as jewel-like and splendid as heavens and into realms that were sinister hells, submerged not in the earth but in layers of dark energy. I found planets akin to mine and I even discovered a person who looked to be my duplicate, as though a twin spirit. It was mesmerizing, but as soon as I gained momentum, all shape stretched out and vanished. Then I was staring into a vortex of innumerable rings of light, the heart of which was blinding white. And then the force released me and I spun weightlessly in a vacuum, conscious without sensation, possessing no sense except of my mere existence within the non-existence of the void. I found myself approaching what appeared to be a mirror, a mirror endlessly surrounding the void. As I approached, my consciousness joined with it and as a result the entire void was lit with consciousness. And then I woke to find I was contemplating the ceiling again.

The epilogue to all this was that I became subject to frequent out-of-body experiences. Awareness was not anchored in my nerves and brain as it had once seemed, so there was a peculiar sense of mind being slightly apart from the physical body during the day, and at night I just drifted out of my sleeping form, hovering near it in the room. I had no sense of a subtle form apart from the physical or what has been referred to as an astral sheath; rather, I was just a point of awareness and mind independent of body. There was no pattern to these events, as they occurred both within and outside dreams, late at night or just at sleep's onset.

These events were intensely disquieting, as it was this separation that had inaugurated my death experiences. I worried that I would again be plunged into the current of the death and would resist it, blindly attempting to struggle to the surface of consciousness. I could not imagine where the next such episode might lead or what it might induce in me. And I was convinced that during any of these death experiences I might reach a point from which there was no return. I compared these experiences to my near-drowning as a child and what I presumed about death then, but had not yet formed a coherent portrait. Whether death was benign or terrible had not been resolved for me. Perhaps these experiences were even a continuation of the death process that was initiated when I had almost drowned; perhaps even a death pattern in me had been permanently unlocked.

Studies on the subject of near-death episodes had just begun appearing, the majority of them induced by harm to the body and cessation of life signs. All of them extended more and less deeply into what death represented, but none of them shed light on what had happened to me. For what precipitated these death events I read about was not significant to me; rather, I was compelled to look at the depth achieved. Many of the experiences just reported standing apart from the physical and looking down on the attempts to resuscitate, which to me were no more than out-of-body or astral travel set into motion by extreme physical duress.

Eventually there were episodes when I was seized by the current of death when outside the physical, but found that if I quickly willed a return to my sleeping form, this current at the core of death vanished just as abruptly as it was met. I had not yet found the heart to pass into and explore death.

The books I happened across were on spiritualism and the occult. I became acquainted with their metaphysical speculations, to which I could not relate. They seemed too impractical, too explicitly magical in connotation. Nor did they illuminate what had been happening to me.

My art work became a vehicle for my search. I even painted a human figure in a vortex of death, his arms outstretched to embrace his ordeal. I became particularly fond of arranging these experiences in whirls of chalk. I looked back upon my childhood drawings, realizing they were much like the representations of mediaeval labyrinths and the mandalas indigenous to spiritualist ritual. I recalled the Jacob's ladder drawings and a secret route by which to reenter death. Well, perhaps I had reentered death, but there was even more required of me in that I needed not to just assemble or map, but to reform and adjust my consciousness until it was suited to such a passage. Our curriculum in fine arts did not permit abstract works; we were learning a craft to later be adapted into an art, so my attempts to recreate my death experiences in paint were not looked upon favorably. For me paintings were no longer a vehicle for a career; painting was just a form of expression I was in need of, which is where it had begun, fifteen years before.

Concurrent with my out-of-body experiences were a number of sensations. A hum had been established in my spine, like an instrument resonating. Voices beckoned to me from the perimeter of hearing; when I lay down there was a pleasant swaying, as though I were in a great sling. I began noticing colored, percolating auras surrounding objects. On a particular night, I stood before my bathroom mirror and saw my entire aura, intense and in motion, radiating bands of light, brightening and dimming, pulsing with emotion and thought. The entire aura spread out and receded, a sea of light reflecting my moods, my thoughts translated into images or mental pictures. It was apparent that thought is energy first and that our primal language is written in bands of light. It was also apparent that we are constantly transmitting our nature across entwining fields of energy and that we live within the spiritual "atmosphere" we have authored. And I learned much about the subject from a book by Leadbeater, a spiritualist from the first half of the twentieth century and a founder of Theosophy; a month prior, I would have strongly denounced him as a fraud.

I assumed initially that my out-of-body experiences would guide me along a course, but I found them to be events without interior wisdom, just compounding the mystery. I continued to search through the occult literature for an explanation, but found what I researched just embroidered the edge without entering the province of my death experiences. Whatever was compelling me was a hollow motion, without heart or deep design.

The more I opposed these energies, the more I was propelled by them into turbulent moods and a jumble of anguished conjectures. Continuing to work nights at the hospital, recommitted to my painting, writing verse in my spare hours, I was settled in a spacious, quiet home with Kathy and yet could not brush past the sense of hopelessness that saturated my days. Even when I was not pondering their riddle, the energies intruded upon my life, coursing through me.

And there were good reasons to be disturbed, for the death experience had a dark undercurrent. Death was not just a matter of survival or rushing toward God; there were hints that death was a test that had to be subjectively mastered. Death was neither a mere passing on nor the act of being snuffed out, but was a process of transmutation of energies. If we were separate from these energies then it would seem we were being annihilated, but if we were wedded to them it would be apparent that we were being transformed. Much would be required of me; I would have to be considerably more prepared for the real death, a death that even if its terminal point was God, it was not the God we had dreamed of and would have preferred. If there had just been the initial death experience I might have been lulled into a pleasant expectation of death's reward. My experience was that death was not just a benign transition but a process in which God may remain hidden.

I noticed, too, that as I encountered my death experiences I had not just observed them; I had become them. Which was just as true of out-of-body experiences—we are a continuance, but not the same person when out of body, just as we behave unexpectedly in dreams. When I examined the matter with care, it became apparent that life and death were of the same design, for life is a transition over decades from a person with whom we are familiar toward one whom we have never met; death manages such a transition in a single leap. Death was not the naive continuation I had longed for. But then mere continuation never exists. We change and are changed again more rapidly than we are capable of mindfully registering. Negotiating death would require poise issuing from such a deep surrender that no distress could uproot it. I would have to be wise in ways I had yet to imagine. I doubted that I could just submit to death again, enduring it without struggle, which perhaps was the ultimate form that wisdom could take. The process I had met with was not just a delirious meeting with God or a motif of passage, but was a divine test, requiring a repolarization of all that we believe and accept. There is no description that adequately expresses what it was like for a mind to be grasped by this momentum. In a small bookshop in a rundown section of town I happened across W.Y. Evans-Wentz's compilation of *The Tibetan Book of the Dead*. Though I did not fully appreciate its ageless wisdom then, assuming it to be a shaman's handbook full of folk deities, I did find a valuable clue. The book emphasized that images are unconsciously projected when we are freed of the body, which I found during my out-of-body experiences: what the mind is projecting and what is actually occurring are interwoven, into a single pattern. This is apparent too when accounts of near-death experiences are examined, because the images representing the light are the sum of what is expected and found most reassuring.

This concept explained to me the difference between the near-death events that were reported and what I had experienced. Any death or near-death event summons up the depths of the mind, the images of which are instantly projected upon the experience. We are literally turned inside out at death. Even a twin likeness of the human body is usually seen, for according to our deepest assumptions we cannot exist without a physical form. But if a person is predisposed to calm acceptance he is less prone to projecting what he expects upon the after-death state.

By what seemed inspired accident, I discovered a book that did provide reassurance and an account of a genuine spiritual process. I was passing through the college library when I was attracted to a shelf, which I approached almost unconsciously, my hand drawn to a particular section as though it were a divining rod. I removed a book with a plain white, worn grass cloth cover. I opened it without reading the title and across from the title page was the photograph of a man with a doe-like gaze and cropped white hair and beard—the Sage of Arunachala. I thumbed through the pages, examining each photograph with care. My breath quickened, my heart flooded with images of the sage as tears welled up. There was a picture of Arunachala as well, a small mountain of consolidated light born upon the dust plains of southern India. Hunched over this biography of Ramana Maharshi, I learned in the final chapter that he had passed on just months before I was born. We would not meet, not ever—that was the thought that swept through me as I slumped to a bench, having read no more of the account than his death from cancer.

I was drawn into the pages, Arthur Osborne's portrait making it seem as though I were a witness to the events so lovingly described. According to the account, he had been born in south India in the village of Tiruchuli in December of 1879 and seemed normal growing up, though at the age of seventeen he had a spontaneous death experience—and as a result he was permanently enlightened. This death was plain and simple, without images or passages. He was in his room alone when he was overwhelmed with the fear of death. He stretched out on the floor, teeth clenched, his breath held, determined to examine the nature of death. He examined all the elements of what he was and, according to his own words, all that was perpetual within him was immortal consciousness. "I am immortal consciousness," he declared. "All these," he later explained, "were not idle speculations. They went through me like a powerful, living truth that I experienced directly, almost without thinking. The fear of death was permanently extinguished. From this time on I remained fully absorbed in the Self," which from his account was a consciousness like a transparent diamond, formless and yet perfectly radiant.

It was about six weeks before I left Madura for good that the great change in my life took place. It was quite sudden. I was sitting alone on the first floor in my uncle's house. I seldom had any sickness, and on that day there was nothing wrong with my health, but a sudden violent fear of death overtook me. There was nothing in my state of health to account for it, and I did not try to account for it or find out whether there was any reason for the fear. I just felt "I am going to die" and began thinking what to do about it. It did not occur to me to consult a doctor or my elders or friends; I felt that I should solve the problem for myself, then and there.

The shock or fear of death drove my mind inwards and I said to myself mentally, without actually framing the words: "Now, death has come; what does it mean? What is it that is dying? This body dies." And I at once dramatized the scene of death. I lay with my limbs stretched out stiff as though rigor-mortis had set in and imitated a corpse so as to give greater reality to the enquiry. I held my breath and kept my lips tightly closed so that no sound could escape, so that neither the word "I" nor any other word could be uttered. "Well then," said I to myself, "this body is dead. It will be carried stiff to the burning ground and there burnt and reduced to ashes. But with the death of this body, am I dead? Is the body I? It is silent and inert but I feel the full force of my personality and even the sound 'I' within me, apart from it. So I am spirit transcending the body. The body dies but the spirit that transcends it cannot be touched by death. That means that I am deathless spirit."

All of this was not dull thought; it flashed through me vividly as living truth which I perceived directly, almost without thought-process. "I" was something very real, the only real thing about my present state, and all the conscious activity connected upon the body was centered on that "I." From that moment onwards the "I" or Self focused attention on itself by a powerful fascination. Fear of death had vanished once and for all. Absorption in the Self continued unbroken from that time on. Other thoughts might come and go like various notes of music, but the "I" continued like the fundamental sruti note (monotone persisting through a Hindu piece of music) that underlies and blends with all other notes. Whether this body was engaged in talking, reading or anything else, I was still centered on "I." Previous to that crisis I had no clear perception of my Self and was not consciously attracted to it. I felt no perceptible or direct interest in it, much less any inclination to dwell permanently in it.[1]

Ramana Maharshi secretly moved to a temple nearby and then to Arunachala, this mountain a holy chord within his enlightened consciousness. From the day of his death experience forward, he remained calmly dwelling in this "Self," which is the support of the universe. Later, when hiking the slopes of Arunachala, he experienced a second death which deepened and expanded his realization to include the world. The world and his self were wedded, of an identical conscious nature. This death experience involved a stoppage of heart and breath and was more like the currently reported death experiences, though he was not just consoled and informed, he was transformed at the roots of conscious being.

All of this was reassuring and, I was convinced, equally unattainable. He had been transfigured by his experience into a wise and immovable saint. I was as deluded and small-minded as I had been prior to my death(s). Not only was I unenlightened, I was perplexed by what had been and was happening. Even more daunting was the fact that I could not decipher Ramana Maharshi's spiritual advice.

My marriage had been completely overtaken by the spiritual search; I had no passion except for the spiritual. Kathy, perhaps expecting that I would become disillusioned and return to her, never objected, but rather seemed to slip inexplicably away from me.

Within weeks of discovering Ramana Maharshi, I was on a train bound for New York City, where I roomed in a cheap hotel and rummaged arcane bookshops such as Weiser's, lugging home paper sacks of spiritual books, most of them with rough paper, cheap ink, and the board bindings of the Indian continent. It was a trip that would be repeated frequently as I explored and charted a spiritual terrain of hope and transcendence. As I read across the spectrum, I became acquainted with the concept of *kundalini*, a framework for spiritual energies normally dormant within the human body but the pole star for all spiritual experience. Kundalini yoga is a nontraditional form of meditation developed in the fourth and fifth centuries, appearing in Jainism, Hinduism, and Buddhism almost simultaneously. Traditionally, kundalini is looked upon as an energy dormant at the base of the spine, usually translated as "serpent power," its image rendered as that of a coiled snake. As long as the energy is coiled up, spiritual life is unexpressed. When aroused spontaneously or awakened through Tantric techniques, this subtle light, or *prana* (life breath), ascends the spine, passing through wheels of energy or *chakras*, which when roused from their slumber and unfolded are metaphorically drawn as lotuses. With each awakened lotus, a spiritual dimension opens. The energy is intensely sexual and primal in nature, originating from a matrix at the root of the sexual organs and dependent upon the same subtle light. The number of chakras agreed upon ranges from seven to nine, with the root of the kundalini looked upon as the first and the terminal point of the energy as a thousand-petaled chakra that crowns the head.

I did not at this point relate the kundalini to the process I had been enduring since I was a mere child, for the descriptions within the Indian texts were too glorious and metaphorical for me to fathom—I considered my experiences to be odd, even absurd—perhaps even hallucination. I assumed kundalini was a myth and the colored paths upon the charts of lotus chakras and presiding deities and descriptions of ascent to be a metaphor for a spiritual attainment that needed to be orally deciphered by an adept in the art of kundalini.

I could find no philosophies that I could surmount and trust amid the wisdoms of India and would have abandoned the project if the lessons on death were not so abidingly with me. Against the panorama of death, the world's passage was quaint and unremarkable, almost not worth notice. I was being pursued by death up a grueling path that I would not have otherwise chosen. The death experiences had provided me with a secret link, more real to me than what I plainly sensed, more intimate and precious than a wife, more sustaining than the art work which had defined me.

Ordinary events were a motion within a fading spectrum that I was both attracted to and repulsed by, fleeting and repetitious, whereas only God represented undiluted sweetness. It would occur to me later that I was perplexed by the range of experiences, that I had experienced too much to make sense of. I had seen into aspects of shamanism and kundalini, far too much to account for, and the more I looked into these subjects the more tangled they became.

Imitating Ramana Maharshi was not a task I was remotely capable of, as his state of deathless abiding seemed to become ever more elusive. Meditating upon and inquiring "Who am I," as he recommended, served just to stir up more energies, energies that throbbed in junctures I had seen mapped out as chakras. Here now was a connection with the ancient energy of kundalini. Yet there was no constant, no pattern that I could anticipate: the energies, in their alchemical churnings, numbed or sensitized, inspiring me to giddiness or rage. In the areas of the lower chakras tender rashes erupted. In the region of the navel I endured bouts of intense burning resulting in repeated hospital stays for a malady that was never diagnosed; on the chart of kundalini this was the site of *manipura chakra*, or the fire chakra, and is associated with the upward movement of vital energies.

Luminous scenes changed and unfolded before my mental gaze when I rested, accompanied by energies that saturated my nerves and made it impossible to achieve a decent night's sleep. Perhaps I would not have minded being governed by the kundalini's powers, but no wisdom or kindness had been born of them, no perfection or godliness—I possessed less, not more, of these qualities. At my core I was burning and so I reeled about and thrashed blindly, needing to harness these energies and defend myself against them by hardening my ego, especially toward those I loved. I raged against those near to me, especially Kathy, though in retrospect it was plain that what I resented most deeply was that I could not be helped—Kathy's love could not touch this torment. I grew more withdrawn, writing poems constantly, the flame of the energies producing them. My ego had to expand continually to keep up with and harness the energies and upheavals to which I was constantly subject. Kathy could not reach out to me because I was impossible to find, for what was happening to me remained largely unexplained. And I could not permit myself a moment's weakness at this juncture, for I was assailed night and day. My ego was continually at war with nightmare and madness.

Chapter Four

Awakening to the World

*Spirits are planted
on this earth;
we become tangled
in distant galaxies,
pour with the rains,
and sing God's praises
whether we hear the
song or not.*

Within months I was saved from this madness as a result of a drawing class. The signs of kundalini subsided, not to appear again for more than a year.

Much of the curriculum at the Wright State College of Fine Arts was scheduled in a great hull of a barn in the woods at the rear of campus. This is where paintings were composed in classes that stretched over long hours. Under the tutelage of a staff comprised of New Yorkers trained entirely on the East Coast, we were exercised in a strict classical style and painted nothing but nudes and still lifes—the unencumbered space of a landscape reserved for the more profusely gifted. Technique was being pounded into us by a staff that was ruthlessly critical, so that the classes were serious, quiet journeys with paint.

On a particular day in late spring of 1971, I was sketching a still life comprised of a ceramic pitcher, a bowl of nodding flowers, and shriveled fruits on a bare table. I propped my easel in a corner of the room. Recently I had acquired the habit of smoking and did so incessantly. I glared at the rest of the class, for I had become impatient with the entire affair of painting, of all the pretenses and aspirations that it involved. Diligently I had worked on the subject all week but could not find the exact approach that suited me. Usually I was preoccupied with space, penciling across the page and then describing the object according to space's dictates. But I had been muddling about, endlessly penciling in and revising the objects on the table, over thinking what usually came naturally. The page had become a maze, the objects ice-like from repeated erasures. In disgust I retreated from my easel to view the jumble from a fresh perspective. As I did so, I suddenly "woke up." Key to this awakening, as though from a protracted dream, was a sense that a lock behind my eyes had opened and I was seeing perfectly what lay before me. It was as though I had been walking through clouds for ages and had just emerged, my eyes suddenly unencumbered.

I examined my state in an attempt to account for it, for it seemed as though I had stepped into what was for a painter a miracle, the things of the room so intimate and close, the light pouring into the windows firing each of them with glorious color. Even the raw space of the room possessed a texture and light. I was returning to my senses as though I had been banished from them, as though I had just been experiencing their wake, never approaching them except across the path of my former trance. I rushed to the instructor, expecting that this was the event that he had been urging upon us. Gushingly I told him that I was seeing, that I had finally awakened and I thanked him, but it was immediately apparent that he was neither prepared for my approach nor had an inkling of what I was communicating—so I walked out of the harbored room into the spring day.

Unprepared for the full-blown beauty of a sunny day late in spring, I stumbled forward along a stream that skirted the barn.

I waded the stream and raced up a hill into the shade of trees. I remarked out loud that I must have found Eden, for regardless of where I looked there was a bonfire of sacred light. I passed over the hill and deep into the woods, happening upon a log, where I settled to examine my state, searching for the element that had been added. But it was soon apparent that it was not what I had acquired, but rather what had been subtracted from me that accounted for my awakening. My mind was not present, not as I usually conceived of it. I was fully capable of engaging in thought as I was upon this subject, but the intimate, endlessly chattering voice that was the twin of my speaking voice was not present. My mind was hauntingly quiet when not called upon; even then there was not the usual over-friendly, emotionally engaging voice. There were no drawn-out exchanges or commentaries; thought was precise and quick.

Prior to this, when I had looked at objects I had not nakedly seen them; between us were the litany of the mind's prejudices and conceits. The senses were dimmed as I stepped back from what was presently occurring. I had assumed that there was no awareness without thought, as though thought made up the edifice of awareness, but I now saw that I had been mistaken, that a mind without thought was more acutely aware. And even more startlingly, I had discovered that "my" voice, with all its undercurrents and emotional tones, was dispensable.

I remained in the woods for hours, purely enjoying the link that existed with nature. I had been returned to the primeval wonder of my childhood. Finally I hiked to where my car was parked and meandered home on country roads across bare cornfields and gentle hills. My senses remained nakedly aware throughout the evening and that night it seemed as though the whirling contentment of crickets on the lawn mixed with the night's breeze provided me with a pleasant, almost unworldly sleep. In a few days my state gradually returned to normal. But I had learned that we are habitually and unconsciously estranged from our senses. Much was explained about human behavior—if we remain apart from and estranged from what is

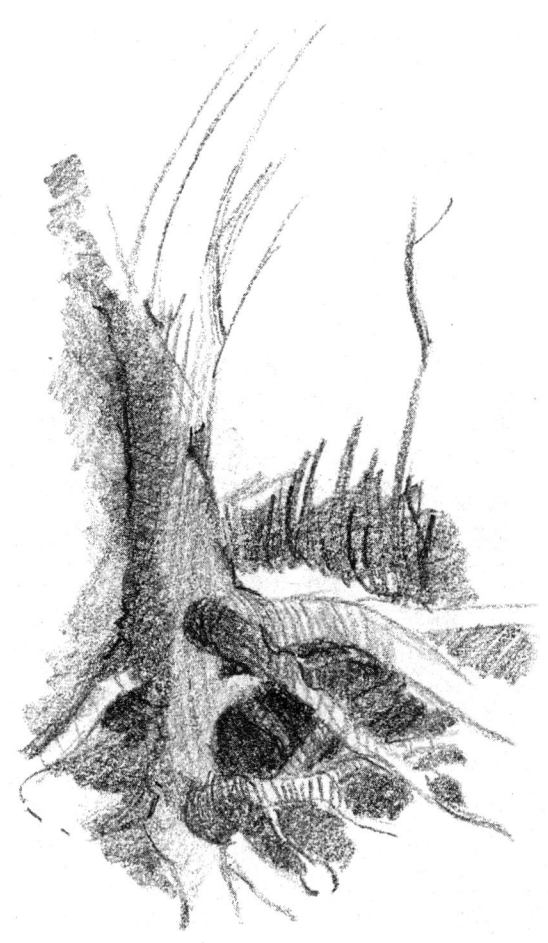

outside us then we are much more capable of being prejudiced and harmful. That which is outside us is more sharply defined as separate because we are perpetually inverted upon our minds. Once that voice is stilled, it is apparent that we are more flowing than we would have ever suspected, with no boundary drawn around us. We are not minds or the mere echo of voices, but are citizens of the world.

But this "waking up" was so natural, so peacefully unlike what I had grown used to that I assumed I had found what I was seeking, that I just needed to practice and cultivate it. I had arrived at a turning point as well in that I decided I would never again pursue what was expected. Because of this awakening, I had seen into, had seen through, the round of human affairs. Even the most rational person existed as a disembodied voice, as though a spirit not anchored in nature, incapable of noticing that the present is not just parading across the senses but is wondrously moving through them.

In the beginning, these ideas were disjointed, fragments that I compared and shaped whenever the experience of awakening was repeated. I kept a journal, assuming that my trials were approaching their conclusion, and perhaps if I had been capable of being so spiritually simplified they would have been. But there was much in me that needed to be addressed and much more that needed to mature and grow wise. It would take me decades to accept that the transcendent is not subject to our will—it cannot be achieved.

Over weeks, the episode faded and my former preoccupations returned, although as a benefit of the experience I had acquired the talent of emptying my mind at will. As the effects of the kundalini ceased, and I engaged in quieting the mind's chatter, I found a steadiness and repose that I was in desperate need of, though there was much more about my typically human condition that needed to be penetrated and learned, particularly since I viewed death as an ordeal requiring that I be thoroughly prepared. So I continued seeking, though I soon confined myself to reading and correlating what I had discovered with what D.T. Suzuki had repeated for most of the decades of this century. I began scouring the land for a Zen roshi as a guide, and adopted a habit of formal sitting meditation. I found this excruciating, for my legs have an inborn defect that no amount of stretching unbinds. But, no matter, in the pose suggested in the Zen manuals I regularly meditated.

Chapter Five

The Net of Kundalini

*A pilgrimage is just
a weight on the tongue,
unless the breath
has truly stopped.
Our awareness thick with light,
the Lion of Brahman on our breath
the birthless honey pouring out
of our hearts.*

In the autumn of 1971 I became involved with a budding spiritual community in Cincinnati, no more than an hour south of Dayton, whose teacher had studied at a Taoist monastery and then had set off to look for illumination in India. Prowling among the saints in India, he became enlightened and returned to Cincinnati under the banner of a guru he helped ordain in America.

The leader's teachings were based on the *Tao Te Ching*; he asserted that all spiritual advice ever needed was within its pages.

His teaching was such a complement to what I had begun seeking on my own that I began faithfully meditating as he described—looking at the mind and attaching no special importance to its workings, allowing enlightenment to naturally occur. After months, I was adept at quieting the mind but doing so did not produce the results I expected. When I quieted the mind it became a stonelike quiet, as though I were staring into my sleep from the outside. I found that even though the mind was silent it functioned just as it always had, that it was even possible to speak from that silence. Resting in that silence when speaking and acting, I found that the kundalini remained dormant and I felt more sane and even marginally matured.

During this period, my marriage became a quiet refuge even though Kathy, as ever, just looked on as I experimented spiritually. Gradually, I became less preoccupied and actually briefly began to share in the rhythms of a normal marriage. Only then was it plain to me all that Kathy had endured and the patience and love I had wrung from her. But because of the energies that were slumbering and were about to reappear with more vigor than ever, the marriage that should have sustained us was about to end almost as it began.

Through a series of events, my involvement with the community evolved into a different group, with me as a leader of sorts, a provider of kundalini. When we meditated as a group, what occurred defied all explanation—in response to the attention placed upon me, not only was the kundalini aroused but it was transmitted to the students. Unmistakable currents of kundalini energy irrigated my spine and bathed the nerves in a just-perceptible glowing radiance. With the energies moving not just in me but also among the students, it seemed, as I spoke, that the kundalini spoke through me. These were ecstatic utterances under the kundalini's influence, rambling across spiritual boundaries, as much concerned with Zen or Taoism as the tantricism from which kundalini originated.

There was a natural form of meditation I was drawn into, a primal rhythm of energy that was in tune with the flux of breathing. It depended upon me expelling energy along with my outbreath, which was then drawn in by the students as they inhaled. In the fleeting gap between breaths I just relaxed into a spaceless quiet, but with the start of each breath I drew into me a source of energy that was pressing on me from above. This energy descended with the rest of the inbreath along the front axis of the body until it reached its lowest point, usually at the root of the sexual organs, though it occasionally turned upward and stopped at the base of the spine. Then there was exhalation and the energy rushed up my spine, along the back of my head or through the middle of my head, resonating against my palate, moving from my eyes into the students. Or I just attempted to breathe in the energy that each student exhaled, circulating it and returning it to them magnified by the transaction. The energy, by nature, seemed to be patterned to both circle in the body and return either to its source above the head or be shared, or exchanged in a conversation of bare energy.

The entire affair was quite peculiar, but exceedingly pleasant, and we would become drunk with it. Initially there seemed no purpose to it, but I began poring over texts on kundalini and attempted to put into practice what I discovered. When I engaged in more purposely surrendering, permitting spaceless energies that loomed over my head to penetrate and freely rule me, there was a leap forward. Currents of lush energy etched the chakras or struck chords of sweetness beneath the sternum at the heart. Soon the experiences were more varied and meditations were held frequently as our meetings attracted more visitors.

I was looked upon as the leader and provider of kundalini for this small group that in turn relied on the energies for guidance. Months passed and the meditations were more formally arranged. There were those among the group who wanted to organize and publish, to push the perimeters of what we were doing. Most would have agreed to any request I made, but I was not prepared to expand. I regarded the kundalini as the proprietor of the splendor of enlightenment. The sacred energy could not be owned by a person; it had to be surrendered into, accepted on its own terms with trust in the work of its secret fires. When the breath was held and the mind was absolutely still, energies poured into me; phenomena would appear, but the nature of my work was just to receive these energies. I was resolute in keeping my mind on this work and not the work of popularizing the kundalini. Besides, I had been warned by the words of the adepts that kundalini was a dangerous passage. I was just a human forge, breathing in and breathing out energies that were perpetually transformative.

I made a trip to New York in the autumn of 1972 and returned by train with a dozen books on kundalini. I compared and learned much about the *shakti*, or energy, of kundalini, its tremendous beauty and power permeating and animating all appearances. In a human being it trickles unnoticed up the spine, but when brought to consciousness it can become a flood, its sacred imprint within the human body flowering. As a result we are, as its faithful practitioners claim, gradually ennobled and translated into spiritual beings.

What was even more striking was that from the evidence I acquired in New York, the kundalini had apparently been awakened in me when I was a child; that the host of childhood experiences to which I had been subjected were a result of this. Initially I had surrendered mindlessly to the energies, but gradually I had attempted to suppress them, more and more uncertain of what these unquenchable energies intended. I had grown up in the shadow of the belief that these energies were not normal and therefore I was not normal. Until this juncture I had never welcomed or mindfully surrendered to the kundalini process.

What was most astounding was that I learned that the ultimate rite the kundalini performed was to raise its energy, along with the human entity, out of body, returning them both to their source: God. I read that kundalini can be roused in a multitude of ways and can rise to many levels, though to approach its origin it has to depart with such power that the body can actually be incinerated. In a book on the life of an Indian sage of the eighteenth century, I happened upon an account of this full arousal, termed *nirvakalpa samadhi*, which was, note for note, the exact experience I had shared with Elaine. I even read of examples of this samadhi being communicated to a second person, just as it had been to Elaine.

According to most sources, the kundalini begins at the base of the spine and, when aroused through spiritual ardor or practices, ascends, piercing all the chakras until the force, or shakti, reaches the highest locus of ascent, which is the thousand-petaled lotus, or crown chakra at the apex of the head. But according to my experience and more obscure sources I found, the energy actually enters the body through the feet, the circuit passing through the base of the spine in its raging ascent. My experience was, oddly enough, that the shakti pierced the body in the foot, in my case the right foot at the point of the great toe, which explained the effect on my right leg when I first encountered the kundalini. And according to all evidence my first encounter was as a child on the baseball field outside the Pentecostal church.

When I lay in bed, not meditating, the pent-up energy would cause my right leg to quiver and leap about and there would be a surge that acquired momentum as it entered the fundamental chakras. On a couple of occasions, that great toe was even blackened, as though it had been singed. It was soon apparent that there were chakras in the legs and, when I examined my entire body, that there was a multitude of chakras, even at the points of fingers and on the lobes of ears. What the texts were prone to describing and mapping out were just the seven chakras essential to spiritual ascent. I even guessed that the chakras could be moved, that there was no fixed locus and a creative drift might occur during prolonged practice or radical departures in the uses of the shakti energy.

Eventually I decided that kundalini and the near-death experience are of the same nature and that the tunnel usually described in the latter is the passage through the spine. Both, too, depend upon the momentum at the beginning of the process; if the momentum is weak a person just appears in the room overlooking his human body, but if there is a considerable amount of energy there will be an ascent toward subtle realms, or even, as in the case of nirvakalpa samadhi, pure light. We then seem to ascend at death; heaven seems "up there" because the kundalini rushes upward into the head and leaps out. If we are not drawn upward at death we may see light or even speak with forms representing that light, but will not merge with it. Death is then just a stepping off, a point of departure, which depends on the path set before it. So if kundalini is not activated in the course of a life it will be activated at death, the "height" of its ascent depending on what is imprinted upon our energies and the energy habits we have acquired. As they are fond of repeating in the Indian texts, "energy flows with the mind."

Even the internal sounds reported in near-death cases, such as buzzing, roaring, or even celestial melodies, or the tinkling of bells such as I heard when I was nearly drowned as a child, are described exhaustively in the kundalini writings, for the ascending power could be witnessed either in terms of light or "music." And it was now evident that the kundalini had been set into motion when I was quite young and had been manifesting ever since, a process which I had viewed both as radiantly holy and as dark and deathlike.

But in regard to the kundalini's ability to enlighten, I harbored doubts. For the circuit within the body was an engine of experience that often behaved so repetitiously that I wondered if enlightenment was being assisted or impeded by the process. For, although the process of kundalini was constantly moving me, it did not seem to be moving me in any particular direction or toward an event that was summary. It was apparent I had once experienced the summit of kundalini in the nirvakalpa samadhi of my death experience with Elaine; but such an enlightenment could not be sustained except as a state removed from the senses and mind; I was seeking an enlightenment that was never apart from any life experience. Yet I possessed no interior compass except for the kundalini and so was compelled to view these experiences as the spiritual sustenance that would eventually provide enlightenment. Of course, even in the Indian texts, enlightenment has many faces. Yet I trusted and meditated and rejoiced in the direction I received.

My informal community's activities focused more and more on meditation, as the energies were more insistent, demanding their own expression. Permitting the kundalini its transformation, accepting its passage through us without amendment or expectation, became our form of meditation. Sessions usually culminated in a quiet bliss, which unlike the other energies did not originate along the spine but seeped into the nerves as though from a source just outside the body. The bliss seemed to touch upon every structure within and we would pitch about as though intoxicated with its joy.

I was perpetually heated by the kundalini and that winter, and for many subsequent winters, rarely required a coat. Soaking in a bath was soothing, but the heat was never fully alleviated. Out-of-body experiences occurred almost nightly, but I remained distrustful, for on occasion I felt the familiar tug of death, which I managed to elude by willing a return to the physical body. Both in and out of body there was a flood of "music" within that seemed to be stretching my skull from the inside out as though to force it to accommodate. The music could be rude noise, especially when out of body, or of surpassing majesty when in deep meditation. Blown conches announced the deepest states of meditation, behind which there were incomparable choirs performing with such splendid beauty that the notes were like passages from a dream that could not be reconstituted in waking memory. No human melody compared with it. In accord with the music were glorious lights that glowed inexplicably within the middle of the head.

To meditate was a process of "riding" the energy and undergoing sublimation of all that is personal into a divine impersonal nature. I attempted to remain as pure as possible to augment this process, seeking to be attuned to the storms of energy that were the only landmarks. I lived as a renunciate amid the usual routines of a modern era. Archetypal symbols and spiritual personages appeared at the *ajna* chakra, or third eye, goading me inward and upward. And it even seemed as though this chakra was working to overlap the mind and recreate it according to its design. The symbol for this chakra is a point and it is the guiding impulse of the entire chakra system. Like a spreading flame, the ajna chakra slowly encompassed the entire brow, as well as reaching into me to the point in the middle of the head where the light and music were reverberating. From this point the theater of the kundalini-shakti was endlessly spellbinding, encouraging me to swoon into its prodigious energies.

An iridescent blue drop, referred to as a *bindu* in kundalini yoga, began to regularly appear; alluring and even sensuous, it would leap into my field of vision whether my eyes were openly engaged or closed in meditation. The drop tended to leap playfully away, by nature too light and insubstantial to be held in place except by undistracted concentration. Like a lover, the blue drop demanded all of my attention or it was gone just as quickly at it appeared. Perhaps Krishna, the seductive blue-skinned God, was even a metaphor for the bindu. According to Indian tradition this bindu is a "particle or spot," a representation of the universe in an unmanifest form. And this particular bindu was the soul or seed of a human being residing in the middle of the head. On occasion a white bindu or a perfectly formed white five-pointed star would appear in the middle of the drop. On the blue field images of spiritual masters appeared; I once saw Yogananda, the author of *Autobiography of a Yogi* and a pioneer of Indian spirituality in America. He was animate, as though upon a movie reel, behaving joyously.

Yet my breath remained the primary vehicle for the energies of kundalini, the nature of which grew more comprehensive. Frequently I sensed that my body was independently breathing and expanding. Or that my entire body was inhaling a pleasure that was almost too much to endure. Or with a sharp inbreath it seemed as though my entire body would vanish.

As the breadth of the experiences increased, however, I grew less enamored with them and in fact soon became despondent.

They began to seem less and less wonderful and even appeared foolish. What did the ceaseless churning of energies actually accomplish? Was it a sign of accomplishment or just a purposeless flourish of energy? Even if the initial ascent of kundalini was repeated endlessly, what would I have accomplished? Perhaps I was wedded to this fate when I did not seize my opportunity and merge with God in nirvakalpa samadhi. This kundalini process we were party to seemed more and more just a matter of indulgence. And as friends grew more infatuated with the process I grew more disillusioned.

We had developed into a small cult, and I suddenly became disgusted with the entire affair. I wished to shed the kundalini and the idolization of which I was not worthy. Within the week of that realization, I abandoned wife, home, and college, and refused to communicate with former friends. I was both saddened and broken by my experience. I had lost all that I loved within the labyrinth of kundalini, especially my wife. The experience of kundalini had distanced me, while the cult had seduced me and even corrupted what we had shared. I began to think that an enamoring madness was ever lurking within me, this kundalini which sages supposedly transmuted into illumination.

Chapter Six

Choiceless Awareness: The Fire of Bare Attention

> *If only they could be read
> Jesus' footprints are still
> on the Red Sea; and Buddha's
> voice is preserved
> in the stones at Deer Park.*

Just as I became aware that I desperately needed an escape from the exhausting intensity of my search and experiences, I discovered and embraced the philosophy of Jiddu Krishnamurti, the author of *Think Upon These Things* and other books. Krishnamurti had been trained from an early age to become the vessel for the messiah of our present age but had denounced the project just as he was pronounced ready. He spent the remainder of his life preaching an enlightenment without a hierarchy. His message, like the ancient Buddha's, was just to practice a form of bare mindfulness he summarized in the phrase "choiceless awareness."

Krishnamurti's ordeal became an example for me. His message was exactly what I needed at this juncture, and I read more of his books and practiced choiceless awareness just as he described. The bare nature of his practice was perfect for me, exhausted as I was by the churnings of the kundalini and the spiritual pretensions I had practiced. To truly observe according to the framework Krishnamurti had developed, it was necessary to set aside all personal images and expectations. And in order to "see" we must die to the past. As Krishnamurti stated in *The Flight of the Eagle:*

> Always to seek for a wider, deeper, transcendental experience, is a form of escape from the actual reality of "what is," which is ourselves, or own conditioned mind. A mind that is awake, intelligent, free, why should it need, why does it have any experience at all. Light is light, it does not ask for more light. The desire for more "experience" is an escape from the actual, the "what is."[2]

I also decided I needed to become socially engaged, that I didn't have a counterweight against my urge to plunge inward. I practiced karate with a friend, muting the kundalini. I was trained as an Emergency Room Technician at Children's Hospital and enrolled in a Paramedics' course in 1973. During this time I wandered through a series of intimate relationships, searching and learning but never satisfactorily nurturing a partnership. Gradually, as I regained my senses, my wanderings led me to Dee, and we began an affair which would repeatedly disjoin and mend over the next decade and a half, all the while remaining passionate and sentimental—for we seemed to be spiritual passengers on the same journey. Our relationship, though, grew slowly, over the heat of shared passions, developing into love over the course of years.

I became outspokenly critical of spiritual authority and, as Krishnamurti recommended, endeavored to observe without expectation. Krishnamurti's path echoed my awakening before the still life and I diligently practiced. His journals and talks were bare and almost harsh in their tone, providing the listener no mere point to grasp. They were probing, working to awaken the listener to the present. We are selfish and act blindly because we have never examined our conditioning or the nature of mind itself. Krishnamurti insisted that in order to remedy this we need to be in touch with the present, shedding the projections and habits we have blindly accepted.

These were conclusions, upheld by practice and considerable thought, which have remained with me. I assumed that my need to experience oddities and miracles had been purged. I was content merely to practice, wedding my mind to the silence that was the harvest of being aware, as Krishnamurti wrote in *Meditations*:

> A meditative mind is silent. It is not the silence that thought can conceive of; it is not the silence of a still evening; it is the silence when thought—with all its images, its words and perceptions—has entirely ceased. The meditative mind is the religious mind—the religion that is not touched by the church, the temples, or chants.[3]

Gradually it was made plain to me that when we casually refer to "mind" we are just referring to what is on the surface. Each thought is supported by deeper thoughts and emotions, by a hidden nature we are never in touch with. To meditate as Krishnamurti was urging was to lay the mind bare, so that the mind is quiet not because thought is suppressed, but because it is acutely aware of itself.

Prior to this understanding I had quieted the mind by just preventing consecutive thoughts from linking, by putting attention on the space between thoughts. Normally our thought patterns seem to blend, so that we are not aware that mind has a silent aspect. Krishnamurti was not suggesting such a technique; he was demanding that we just nakedly observe, so that the mind is not just quieted, but is awake and responsive.

Within the mind I found numberless subtle motions that could not be extracted as image or thought. And when these motions were at rest the mind possessed a native glow, a repose that was intensely pleasurable. This glow was an aspect of the meditation which I overlooked, for I distrusted all that was connected with light and so looked past it, gradually submerging all concepts and reasons in choiceless awareness.

As the months passed, gradually attention acquired a bareness that permitted me to see that I was not independent, but was embraced by and founded upon all the intersecting events of a perpetual present. I truly had no separate past that was less than the history of all that was. I was entirely humbled for I was a link in a harmonious process and not a subject standing apart. I was not a person; I was a process of interdependence and motion. It was in this most ordinary of practices that I had unearthed a diamond.

I assumed that I had permanently matured into enlightenment. Whichever way I turned, whatever I happened to look upon, I found that I was reflected against the arc of mutual dependence. Yet this dependence could not be directly examined, for it was never distinct from the *act* of experiencing itself. Lessons upon the nature of this interdependence would occupy me for the next decade.

Attention was quietly and pleasantly poured into a coalescing present that bore no resemblance to the rapturous kundalini, which had always been imposed upon normal experience, even, on occasion, to the point of obliterating it. By meditating on the kundalini I had been perpetually fulcrumed *against* the present, but by resting in interdependence I was always arriving *into* and embracing the present. As Krishnamurti was so fond of repeating, "we are the world." The simple practice was to remain ever standing at the heart of being. On the subject of interdependence, Dogen, the greatest Zen sage of Japan and founder of the Soto sect, once wrote in *The Universal Book of Eternal Peace*:

> In the third month of spring
> the fruit is full on the enlightenment tree;
> One night the flower blooms
> and the whole world is fragrant.[4]

This realization deepened, instilling with it an unshakable poise. I needed to be neither thought-full nor thought-free, but just linked to a present that was ever at the crest of a wave. Cultivating this meditation brought about yet more changes in lifestyle. I isolated myself from all former relationships. Through the mid-seventies, only Dee remained my link to the practical world, balancing my extremes, providing constant support. I worked nights and meditated in the morning and woke up about noon to meditate again before again napping. I meditated in bed or on the bare floor, heaped in blankets in winter, for the heat in my boardinghouse room was, at best, inconsistent.

My primary work became to bind each task I performed in the course of a day to choiceless awareness. My role as Emergency Technician at Children's Medical Center was abolished, but I was not devastated; most of what I had formerly cherished and hoped for was gladly surrendered as I practiced and experimented with attention. I just needed work that was undemanding and marginally provided for my needs—so I asked to be reassigned as night clerk at the hospital. Months passed almost without being noticed and I was content to be poor, with old cars that frequently broke down along the highway and clothes picked out of bins at Goodwill. Dee, my opposite, was conscientious, poised, and exquisitely dressed. People were astounded that we were a couple and repeatedly inquired about the unconventional nature of our relationship.

The wisdom which had gradually appeared over the past four years healed an entire life, as the present was ever breathing within me and conspiring to make me happy. It was a glorious period.

I was preparing to travel, to examine and perhaps plunge into a Buddhist community that practiced the art of mindfulness. I abandoned solitude and I stepped out into the present, the shape of my realization coincident with whatever I discovered. A link had been permanently forged that would remain the foundation of my meditation for the rest of my life.

I concluded that each human being is molded according to the dictates of social order and we spend the remainder of our lives attempting to mend the damage incurred. But if we accept the natural process of mutual dependence, we do not engage in healing but find we have never been sick. We are made sick by the complexities we assume. Human beings can think complex thoughts without becoming complex; we must remain personally simple and linked to nature even as we write the equations of the universe.

But this view was about to shatter, for I was about to stumble out of my realization. I had been making a critical mistake: linking realization to my ego, being seduced by a pride in my attainment. The more remarkable the states and experiences I unearthed, the more inexhaustible my ego became. Because of this, my realization would not return for almost two decades, although when it did it was in a deeper and more enriched form.

Chapter Seven

The Law of Suffering

*Do not become bound up in
beautiful scriptures or
wonderful images;
The plain stone of attention
is much more precious.*

Dee heard about a restored Shaker village in Pleasant Hill, Kentucky. I was inspired to study the Shakers and found that I had an affinity for their practical impulses and their "simple gifts" of spirit. Early that spring we decided on a weekend visit. We drove south and once we were in Kentucky the rains raced over us, the trees along the road shaking off their winter stiffness in gusting spring storms. The architecture of Shakertown was as simple and ingenious as I had imagined it. The Shakers had been a prim and judicious folk, but sang and danced madly and mindlessly in their worship. On our second day there, as we walked among exhibits, my senses began dimming and I nearly fainted. I had to wrench each breath out from under a great weight. Wherever I turned suffering had suddenly appeared, a suffering that was so sharp and real that I seemed to be impaled upon it. Thoughts were jumbled inside of me and my mind was racing. Among these thoughts was the thought that I had not addressed the suffering that was fundamental to all dependence—I had neither transcended it nor worked to heal it.

I was acquainted with the law of suffering as Buddha had preached it in ancient Nepal and India, but never had I appreciated the plain, harsh nature of it until then. The ancient texts were bare and expressed plainly, but this suffering was more raw and primal than any experience I had ever imagined, the burning root of all existence. There was a burden, never noticed or addressed, within the pit of my heart, against which the entire world was leveraged. We were all suffering, in accord; suffering weighed upon us night and day. This was not simply a rational conclusion, for the pain was the most real and primal that I had ever encountered.

Whatever was happening to me required more energy than I possessed to resist the enormous pressure that gripped me. It was as though all the energy in me was leaking from my heart, spokes of it radiating into space. I realized then that the ego had to be either transcended or consumed; it could not just be harmonized. For the ego was the form that this suffering had taken. But a prospect occurred to me that I had never imagined; to achieve enlightenment for my own sake would be a crime, and even though I would not suffer, suffering would be my legacy. I would be upholding this suffering, for just stepping away from suffering without addressing it was to pass along its thread. Not until I met a remarkable priest several years later, however, would this message unsettle the stone in my heart.

Dee grasped my arm and led me about. It must have seemed to passersby that I was having a stroke or heart attack as I reeled about clutching my chest. She guided me to a porch in the shade and examined me tenderly. I hunched forward, my heart grown so heavy that I could not carry it. As Dee mopped the sweat and fingered my racing pulse, the suffering relaxed its stonelike clench and my heart was again at rest. We walked on, but I was upset and weak and so returned to my room to review what had just happened. My thoughts on the subject kept me up most of the night.

Joy was not the bounty of mutual support and dependence; it was suffering—even if there was no person within who was bearing this suffering, which had been my case, for I had existed at large in suffering and had never been touched by it. I had not transcended suffering. I had just negated the ego that suffered so that I was a shell, a motion that could not contain or hold onto experience. I had just hidden the self within my practice, merging it with my choiceless awareness. By doing so I was avoiding the raw, unpredictable nature of experience, stepping around rather than through the human predicament. I presumed that the Buddha's teachings had warned of this avoidance. The flaw was all too apparent as I stood there with my heart wounded and pouring out. I had sought enlightenment by merging with nature, for nature is always in harmony even as the parts of it are enduring perpetual suffering. But to put on the mantle of this enlightenment was to uphold that suffering, for all about me were entities that were enduring their predicament and blindly perishing—ever subjugated by nature.

Following this experience in Kentucky, my energy was thin and I was continually exhausted, barely capable of functioning. I kept to bed for weeks, working but a couple of days a month. I was permeated with this suffering, just as I had once been with a sense of embracing all of nature. I suppressed the meditation that I had dedicated years to steadying. I decided I desperately needed help and renewed my plans to travel, to seek guidance. Suffering was a message so perfectly described to me by my experience at Shakertown that I was leaning toward finding a refuge in Buddhism.

Within weeks I had planned and embarked on a journey across the country to meet with spiritual groups that seemed most promising. It was 1977 and I would see America and perhaps even endorse a spiritual path and be reinspired. In early summer I purchased a used Pinto with 60,000 miles on the odometer and put a bag of clothes in the back. I had $500.00 in cash, some of which had been supplied by the gambling winnings of a friend. Dee was to accompany me on the leg to New

England. I would return with her to stand up in an old friend's wedding and then head west. I sent out inquiries to spiritual groups and planned my route accordingly.

The journey's first primary destination was Monhegan, an island along the coast of Maine. En route I visited a warehouse in New York City that the Hare Krishnas had decorated as an Indian garden and the ashram of an American guru in New Jersey. At the ashram, I became involved in an argument about the role of a guru, my stance being that the concept of the guru was an image unearthed in a dim past and had no place in the modern present. I argued that the guru's passage is unique and the devotee cannot simply duplicate what the guru has done; there can be a transference of energies (shakti), but not of wisdom. Wisdom must be freshly grafted to our own experience; there is no abridged journey. Chasing the spirit is a hardship requiring a stubborn, mule-like persistence, not a mere romance.

As the debate raged, I noticed that a nearly imperceptible shift had occurred within me. I was recovering from my ordeal—though the sense of connectedness remained, I was able to accept the suffering inherent in it. Gradually it occurred to me that any kind deed would mute the suffering, and I presumed that addressing these devotees honestly was such an act of kindness.

Dee and I drove north, staying for a couple of nights in Boston. I had planned to look into spiritual groups there, but I had not regained my bearings since New York. So we just hiked about, translating the paths on the map into historical districts. Then we drove through the night and arrived in Maine just past dawn, my sense of purpose regained. The sole means of transit to the island of Monhegan was an old mail tug that docked at the village huddling in the cove on the southwest shore of the island. The day was overcast and as we set out a storm stood on the horizon; we made a blind passage against a raging sea, arriving in the village with both us and our luggage sopping. Reputed by sailors of old to be a mammoth whale transformed into a land mass, the island bore just this tiny village and a scattering of shingle houses with only kerosene for light and heat. The middle of the island was saddled with a virgin forest. There were soaring cliffs abutting the wide, frigid sea to the east, and upon the northern coast were seal ledges. A hill at the summit of the island was crowned with a lighthouse standing waist-deep in a nineteenth-century graveyard. The house we were lodged in was no more than a wooden shell, unheated except for a single fireplace on the ground floor. The nights were damp and gusting, and we soon met all our neighbors housed on the grassy plain near the open sea, for we were in possession of the only working fireplace. The people were more enlightened than any others I had met in my travels and we made friends and had many discussions with a couple who studied with a disciple of Gurdjieff in New York City.

My days on Monhegan were spent recovering. I climbed about on cliffs most of the week, happening upon a secret ledge that hung over the sea, but just out of sight of land. I would stretch out there, entranced by sea motion, cloud-raked skies, and skimming gulls. Ducks and seals floated on the ocean swells. On a particularly auspicious day a whale surfaced almost within reach of my perch. I had hoped to be refreshed and resume my former spiritual course, but I was finding the present too wondrous to ignore and so had no mind to spare for such tasks. The shifting seas became my thoughts; this was my profit from all that practice of attention—I was able to utterly sink into what my senses enjoyed. Just a few days into the week, we joined the others on a beach strewn with great stones to watch the sun set. Bonfires were lit and crowds huddled in blankets on plates of rock, a harsh wind skimming the sea. As I stood hugging Dee, a new aspect of suffering presented itself to me. The suffering was indeed endless, but it was also wildly magnificent—this was the essence of it. I had endured the suffering without ranting against it and therefore looked through it and saw that it was exuberant and grand, that suffering was just as magical as the rest of nature, and governed by the same almost magical laws. Suffering existed to heal and instruct;

there was no way to see with the eyes of the heart as I had in Shakertown unless suffering was permitted and even embraced.

That week I went to my ledge each morning, whether it was raining or bright, and relaxed and pondered all that had happened to me up until then and it seemed I was just setting step on the path. At night I gathered with the folks from the neighboring houses by the fire and enjoyed company as I had never before. Dee remained quietly apart from me most of the week, accepting my solitary happiness in the same way that she had accepted my suffering. I napped for hours on the rocks, having amazing dreams even as I heard the wind in my ears, not expecting or needing my enlightenment to return, nor even minding that I was perpetually immersed in suffering.

CHAPTER EIGHT

A Spiritual Wayfarer in the West

*A thousand deaths and a
thousand rebirths are
held in the human heart.
When the heart grows eyes
we see nothing but riches.*

As we had planned, Dee returned home after the eastern leg of my journey, and I headed west. Never had I been so unimaginably happy. I followed no maps and was in no hurry, roaming along the roads that held an appeal, nights spent at the wheel, days reserved for reading paperbacks, napping, and wandering and looking. I slept by sun's light, preferring the mood of the night along the road. The cheap fantasy novels I read, as poorly written as most were, seeped into my dreams, as there was no pull on my consciousness except for the pages I read. For I did not ponder spiritual subjects. I was, for the present, enjoying my lack of purpose.

Gradually the heart's suffering faded, as though I was just emerging from a persistent and strange dream. Whenever I had the chance I frequented the slow, vacant off-roads and paid for a motel if it was not too dear and away from the usual path. My first stop, after just over a week's travel, was the San Francisco Zen Center. Life here was exceedingly regimented, the monk's day carefully parceled out. Zen in practice was not as I had imagined, as I had read too much on the subject not to have been romantically indoctrinated. I expected subtle nuances, then surprised shouts of awakening, an enlightened dance between quiet and ritual. But the monks seemed to be blankly imitative of an ancient past, ingesting the cadence and language of their practices as though it were medicine. Soto Zen looks upon meticulous practice and uninterrupted attention to detail as the structure of enlightenment itself. I imagined an enlightenment that

was more expansive, less formal and rigidly held. Although I admired the practice and what was happening at the center, it was apparent that I needed to be able to inquire apart from a religious structure, to distill spiritual wisdom according to my needs and not according to a path, perhaps hardened with age, of an ancient culture and hierarchy. I had imposed, and would later do so again, just as harsh a regimen upon myself, but it was of my own making and according to my own needs.

Without having so much as heard the roshi lecture, I vanished from the zendo just as quickly and quietly as I had appeared, setting the pattern of all my visits to communities on the West Coast—I had just wanted to observe the human current. The stature or attainment of the guru or roshi was important to me only in the manner in which it transformed the monks and practitioners. So I sat among the faithful and observed them as quietly and diligently as I could.

From there I drove to another community in northern California. This was a prosperous spiritual project that revolved around an American guru who claimed to be representing Ramana Maharshi as well as the Siddhi tradition of India. I encountered in my two weeks there the disillusionment that is a product of guru-worship and was glad to move on. Ten miles way, I rented a cabin on a lake where a disillusioned follower of the guru showed up and remained with me for a couple of days.

Once alone again, I just rested, sitting each day on the lake's bank, never venturing deeper into the bluish pines that hemmed in the cabins than to stretch the legs I kept folded beneath me most of the day. During my sittings I just watched the passage of the day across the lake, for a while neither expecting nor desiring to be more enlightened than this.

From there I drove south along Route 1, to Santa Monica, where I stayed with an old sweetheart with whom bonds of friendship remained. I once again took up my journal, attempting to arrange and edit my thoughts, and in my writings found that I was adept at criticizing and discarding, but not at accepting. So I vowed to search more diligently, even though I had no clue as to what I was searching for. I attended lectures at the Vedanta Society, but the radical, spiritual vigor of Ramakrishna, heir to India's grand spiritual legacy and the inspiration for the society, had been relegated to the past. What I was searching for was a figure like Ramakrishna or the Sufi sage Rumi, on a breathless spiritual pilgrimage through life. I toured a Hindu temple, spent afternoons in Yogananda's prosperous gardens, even had an accidental meeting with a Tibetan lama in a park; but could not find the roar of freedom I was searching for, just polite spirituality.

Finally, after spending a day at the Theosophical Society just outside Santa Barbara, I set a course toward Ojai and the Krishnamurti Foundation, which was but a couple of hours north of Los Angeles. Krishnamurti was not in the country except in the spring, but I happened upon an opportunity to stay at the home of a secretary at the Krishnamurti Foundation. For a month I lived in luxury, my only obligation to walk a pair of retrievers each morning. I strolled the orange grove of the Krishnamurti Foundation and meditated beneath the pepper tree where Krishnamurti reputedly became enlightened.

In the grove my meditation took a course which it would maintain for years. Instead of *emptying* the mind to put attention on what appeared, I fixed my gaze entirely *on* the mind, which was breached by no motion or objects and eclipsed all that was human or personal. There was no space, no form, just an immaterial core that the mind could be conscious of but could not make an object of and examine. This emptiness was utterly subjective; instantly when it was looked upon as an object it vanished—which seemed to confirm that it was my most secret nature. Perhaps it was the serenity, or the lack of all clinging that appealed to me, but this immaculate quiet, which had once repelled me and I had accused of being stonelike, was suddenly irresistible.

I went on to Arizona and New Mexico, but I was no longer searching. My old friend Rick was in Arizona and we spent a couple of days at a hotel atop a mountain along the Mexican border. Rick had married and embarked on a military career; and I was as uprooted and spiritually mad as ever. I had not reported home for almost six months. When I finally phoned Dee and my parents, I found that I was out of work and that Dee had met a man and was not expecting me when I returned.

Chapter Nine

The Mind in Emptiness

Robbed of all but the silence;
All the unimaginable worlds
resting on the point of a diamond
beneath the petals of the heart.

I returned to a cramped upstairs bedroom in my parents' home, remaining for hours on the quiet summit of my meditation. I did not work, but had no outstanding debts, few obligations, and rarely ventured from my room. All I possessed was stuffed in a room, most of it boxed or stacked, the rest of the room no more than a path from the door to a narrow bed.

I did scant reading, depending more on what I gleaned from meditation. The interior quiet has no quality or preferences that can be found except through doing. Because there is no plan or map in an empty mind, only when an act is performed is it plain in what direction that quiet is leading. Because there is no apparent image in the quiet mind, a bedrock trust must be developed. Normally we anticipate, picturing and acting out what we hope is lurking around the bend or fear most will be across our path; but when there is just an empty mind we must trust that we possess the inherent wisdom to react appropriately to what may materialize, without depending on anticipation or habitual judgments.

The quiet or empty mind is not as we imagine and expect when we read the texts of the world's mysticisms. To begin with, it is not the splendor that is usually described, nor is it permeated with bliss. Too many grandiose, misleading terms have been applied to the interior quiet. It is easily approached if we just learn to space out our breaths, and notice that thoughts naturally space out in response. For the processes of thought and respiration are linked; when breath is calm, so is mind. The pauses in our normal thought process tend naturally to coincide with the pauses between inhalation and exhalation. Gradually we will develop a talent for holding onto the thoughtlessness apart from breath. Then it just depends on concentrating on that space until we have become used to the "feel" of the emptiness; and we will just feel the emptiness that is perpetually in mind and no leap or process is required. The empty mind, I noted, was approached as a seeing, as the mind looking back at its own quiet. But there is a duality in seeing, for then the seer must be present along with the seen—the emptiness. When we "feel" the emptiness, this duality is consumed, mind and quiet are utterly merged.

This emptiness is not the mere state of being thought-free. We can have a quiet mind without finding a passage into emptiness, such as when I remained thoughtless in my practice of choiceless awareness. The quiet mind is a state that can be assumed and used—almost all spiritual pursuits depend on thought control, and all forms of extreme concentration depend on suspending the mental dialogue. Artists depend on thoughtless flights of inspiration for their work, and athletes are "in the zone" when there are no mental barriers to their performance. In contrast, true emptiness is what occurs when the mind has moved past all that can be referred to as *experience*. The senses can move, even the mind moves, but the predominant space in the mind is never moved or occupied or even actually experienced—it just is.

As I was quartered in my room for weeks with almost no interruption, my meditation matured. I had no object on which to meditate, not even a subjective quiet. Gradually, memories and dreams were immersed in this emptiness. The emptiness both attracted and repulsed me—for it became a ritual in which I was witness to my own unsupported, insubstantial nature. A trace of awareness remained, but it was just enough for the continuation of emptiness; there was no purposeful witnessing. I had erred previously in not taking refuge in this quiet mind, for now I found when there was no definable being there was no suffering. Gradually made aware that this was not just emptiness but pure being that I was meditating on, I began to trust that eventually I would return from this pure being with all the keys to suffering in my grasp. Finally the portrait that Ramana Maharshi had been painting all his life was penetratingly apparent to me, as in this statement quoted in his biography by Arthur Osborne:

> When in fact the body is in the Self, to think that the Self is within the insentient body is like thinking that the cinema screen on which a figure is projected is inside the figure. Has the ornament any existence apart from the gold (of which it is made)? Where is the body apart from the Self?[5]

But this quiet was exceedingly hard to examine or think over and each insight was hard won; for all examination had to be done in the past, when the experience had been relinquished. I could not actually see either the subject or the mind as experiencer. There was, eventually, not even a seeing, but just awareness with no impression being made upon it. But the empty mind was not just a blank, but a spaceless being and a conditionless core.

Apart from the meditation, I just subsisted. My diet was spare, and I grew almost emaciated and unkempt in appearance, for meditating on this pure being had robbed me of a self-image. I was hired back at Children's Hospital and worked for a meager wage, mopping halls and scrubbing down the morgue when an autopsy had been performed. Eventually I returned to the emergency department and staffed the triage room, taking vital signs and determining the priority of each patient. I worked evenings and when there was a need sat at the clerk's desk. This simple work was easier for me, as I was perpetually engaging the empty mind and was habitually distracted from my duties. The meditation had become a process like peeling an onion—whatever layer the quiet meditation unwrapped, even more subtle states of mind lay below.

The kundalini was still muted; unable to intrude upon or touch pure being, it remained, but just outside my meditation. The form the kundalini took was of pressure and subdued motion working in conjunction with the empty mind. When I meditated on pure being, the experience of kundalini was confined to regions of the head. There was an expanding pressure in the middle of the head, although there was also a sharp prodding against the top of the skull or the sensation of energy arching over the cranium and pouring into the space between the eyes. These motions were not fundamental, however, as they had been when I was meditating on the kundalini; rather, they remained attendant to the concentration on pure being. And once I was entirely immersed in pure being they were muted and distant.

Curiously, I found that I remained more conscious during a night's sleep and that the nature of sleep was not affected by my meditation. Most fascinating was the transition into sleep and the process by which a dream was conjured from disjointed phrases and images flooding up from the unconscious—all night the inner space was rich with both random language and inborn images. But there were dreams as well that did not originate in the mind but seemed to be transmitted from an outside source. They were not plainly formed from the stuff of the mind but just appeared, visually richer and more coherent.

These seemingly foreign dreams would, as my practices matured, be read as signs and heard as guides.

I soon became convinced that the traditional forms of meditation were actually phases of consciousness that correlated with the stages of awareness: waking, dream, and deep sleep. The joining and melding of images and energies in kundalini was akin to dreaming. We flow from sleep to waking when we project our minds on what we encounter in the world, the dreams just as vital to our character but hidden from us. It appeared to me we are ever engaged in a form of dreaming. Passing into deep sleep while in full awareness was just a continuation of my meditation. This was the way it was described in the Vedanta, which supports almost all of Indian philosophy, though prior to this I had assumed the pure being of Avaita Vedanta to be just a religious metaphor. I had encountered such rich symbolism in Indian sutras before, legend and dream layered into tracts upon meditation. Such imagery warmed the dry, inhospitable climates of the nondual philosophy of Vedanta to acquaint us with puzzling concepts. Since the journey to California, I had been keeping a notebook and continually jotted down these insights and comparisons.

The correlation to these rhythms of consciousness seemed to provide a support for meditation. To meditate was then to just willfully look into the natural process that consciousness was continually undergoing. Human consciousness mirrors a deeper order of which we are but vaguely aware, but to which we are ever yoked; an order streaming through our body and mind, though we are mesmerized with the objects existing within these states.

In kundalini I had traced the energies of dreams and the more ethereal aspects of mind. In choiceless awareness, I had expanded the waking mind until almost no dreams appeared and the natural order of my identity vanished. In my present meditation I was distilling all I had learned into pure being. Yet perhaps pure being did not best describe it, for what touched upon all of these states, but was never described or summarized in them, was *awareness*. The core paradigm was not then energies, or a natural identity, but a numinous awareness that had been termed in Vedanta as Beingness or Self, irradiated with invisible wisdom. And I was, again, meditating in bed, remaining there for unnatural stretches, working an occasional evening to provide a nominal rent. I was submerged in the pure being I had found while in California, almost seamlessly weaving deep sleep to my meditation, finding that there was no lesson in all my searching except that that which is without form is permanent.

> Everything is essentially without character, name, or place. The way things seem, or appear, is only brief, or without significance. Each moment is only a configuration, a change across nothingness. Nothing endures, or persists, no matter what one feels, thinks, or speaks. All arguments are riddled with silence, all events are without content. No time, space, or thing is continuous, because it is only moving into, toward, upon, within, around, away from, nothing.
>
> from my Notebook, Ojai 1978

Night and day passed and were hardly noticed as I meditated on pure being; sleep and waking blended into a new, indeterminate shape. It was as though a perpetual metamorphosis of awareness was played out, but not with distinct stages as before. I acquired a room at a boarding house and shuttled back and forth between it and the room upstairs at my parents'. The few evenings I worked more than provided for my sparse needs. As months passed, the awareness within became more vast, more tranquil, more like an inner sea. What would be considered normal dreaming and waking states hardly appeared, and as my awareness plummeted even a sense of being vanished.

Once, this meditation had seemed a mere interruption of the mind's noise, a space between subjective occurrences. And as it steadily evolved it became a form of engagement which rubbed the mind smooth of all sense of dependence or independence; I became a Self that was quietly aloof from nature. Self, as Ramana Maharshi had summarized it, was a motionless being from which the world emanated. But this Self stood apart from and was not subject to the world. This was the state into which Ramana Maharshi had initially immersed himself, remaining in trances for days in the temple precincts near to his beloved mountain.

But what I had failed to examine was Ramana's second death experience, which had passed into him while he walked on the mountain of Arunachala, an event that joined his Self to the world. After this event Ramana looked upon the world as resting in the immutable Self. The world then both embraced and was held by the Self. I had yet to penetrate the matter this deeply, though I would gradually achieve this state. But this mistake is easily explained in that I did not possess the spiritual genius of Ramana Maharshi.

Bordering upon pure being was the will. I was surprised to find that the will was not dependent upon the thought process. Will initiates acts without ever referring to thought. The will leaps forward with thoughts lagging after it, claiming and explaining what is prior to the thought process. It was apparent that we not only exist as pure being, but endure in a world of objects as pure intention, or will, acting through the mind and senses.

Chapter Ten

Enduring the Void

*What we forget
we have remembered;
What we have lost
in silence will be
reclaimed with our
true voice.*

As I passed a year in meditation I became more isolated, requiring so little of people I knew that most gradually faded out of my life. My quiet regard of my own nature was too harsh a climate for most people to endure.

But that winter I plummeted into a despair that I would not have thought humanly possible to endure. As I was meditating on a particular evening in January, the wind blowing sharply outside the door and a sole lamp in the room muted with a blanket, my meditation contracted and all depths and nuances summarily vanished. All that remained was a corpse-like, uncaring silence. There was no motion or worth, just a stone of silence in which there was no God and no hope for God. And no Self. And as the days wore on the silence continued to harden, becoming ever more stilling. All that I had endured and discovered over many years now seemed of no purpose. I had finally penetrated the truth—there was no God, no transcendent person, no Self; there was merely a hole into which I had been pouring energies to make it seem alive. This state became almost unendurable as it became painfully clear that all spirituality was a hoax. At the core of all existence was a vacuum that was unbreachable and real.

I began drinking, a habit which I had never before acquired, and became a patron of local bars in an attempt to numb the silence that was ever bearing upon me and the nagging voice in my mind that mocked me for ever having begun the spiritual quest. I was drunk many nights and was smoking again, after years of abstinence. The inner silence was unaffected, bare, without a single human quality or any redeeming warmth. My personality was gradually transformed as well, for whereas I had been quiet and placid I became increasingly scornful and easily angered. When I was not socially engaged or drinking, I felt I was suffocating in a dark and airless ether. I could not hide it or avoid it; the human condition was present within me—a void. I had pursued mysticism, rejecting all prospect of having a home and caring relationships, and what I had gained in return was a profound nihilism.

Many assume that to be immersed in a void is an uncomplicated, quiet release at death—that it is sleep without sleep's pleasant undercurrents. But to remain ever in contact with such a void, night and day, sharing all experience with it, can be almost more than one can bear. I merely endured. I had to speak and act from such a void where there should have been instead life and life's best hopes. And the void was urgently pressing itself upon me, as though it hungered. That which I looked upon as a womb of nourishing quiet was now an all-consuming silence that could not be appealed to, transformed, or suppressed.

Absorbed in numberless regrets, ever picturing what life might have held for me, I was in constant anguish. I regretted I had not had a career in medical illustration, for I had been offered a scholarship in that field. But even more urgently, I wished for a wife and children and all the rote happiness of which I had been so suspicious while spiritually seeking.

A fledgling interest in philosophy led me to befriend a coworker who had earned a master's degree in Western philosophy. Nightly debates ensued, particularly on points of free will and existentialism. When not working, we often met at diners to work out philosophical concepts as allies on the path of reason. I had never before appreciated reason and briefly soared unburdened from my meditation. We were attempting to graft Western reason to Eastern mysticism. I was often amused when he referred to me as the only "genuine mystic" he had ever met.

I was particularly attracted to the existentialist view that life has no meaning apart from what we project upon it. Existentialism seemed to reflect the essence of my meditation, for what I believed I had uncovered about my essential nature was that it was meaningless and vacant. The patron of modern French philosophy, Jean-Paul Sartre, proved most influential to me, as according to him each of us is cut off from the rest of the universe by a nothingness. We are irrevocably made alone by this nothingness, but because of it free will is made possible. We have to be separate in order to possess free will. And this struck me as the same nothingness that was suffocating me.

Although I persisted in my drinking binges, I began lifting weights in a rundown gym, seeking to become as hard and hardened as I could—deciding that I needed to adapt to the harshness of nature and its nothingness. I decided that even the kundalini had been an hallucination; that all my spiritual pursuits had been purposeless and mad. Perhaps when I passed through the unrelenting anguish a mature and wiser man would finally emerge—so even then I had begun to hope.

The next spring I met a woman who would permanently affect me and helped define the purpose my life later found. I first saw her one morning in the old section of hospital, seated in the hall, her auburn hair settled about her like a shawl. She looked like the woman in the kitchen illustration by Maxfield Parrish. Her eyes were brightly cheerful as she reviewed a patient's chart, her thin legs stretching away from her. After working my shift, I returned to inquire about her. The nurse on duty squinted impatiently before pointing along the hall. It was then that it dawned upon me—it had been her own chart in her lap. She was a patient on the ward.

Reading her patient history, I learned that Jill was nineteen; she was an orphan; her parents died when she was sixteen. Just past her seventeenth birthday, she was diagnosed as having an inoperable brain tumor. She was being readmitted to Children's Hospital because this is what she preferred.

I found out more about her from a nurse on the night shift. According to her, Jill was taken to church by a neighbor when she was nine and of her own accord received Christ as her saviour. As a result her entire family became Christians. In the wake of her parents' death in a road accident, the church provided her with considerable support and as soon as she was of age she married a prominent member.

When she was diagnosed with cancer, the entire church was held in suspense and there were prayer vigils lasting for nights until Jill did begin improving and it was announced from the pulpit that she was healed. She was eighteen and just married. But when she relapsed and returned to the hospital, her husband abandoned her. Except for the members of her church, Jill was alone.

When the nurse finished her story, I went to Jill's room and found a woman who was decisive and brave, her spirit seeming to loom fully in her body. Our conversation was tentative and quiet, but when I left that night I had already begun to love her and saw a hope I had not dared imagine a week earlier. I would become a Christian, join her church, heal her with my prayers, prayers than I had begun even then. I was sure that I was gazing with stunning accuracy into our future.

I was surprised with the zeal with which I accepted Christ as my saviour. In a blinding stroke I was redeemed, Christ had taken me over and I had renounced my sins, most just recently acquired. I went to church on Sunday, praying with the assembly in Jill's behalf. Secretly we exchanged rings, as I visited with her just at night, through most of the night. She napped between the barrage of tests and treatments that passed as her day. In our giddiness we even planned a marriage.

But Jill never improved. She grew deaf and nearly blind as her hair fell out from the chemotherapy treatments. A nurse loaned her a cheap wig. Her makeup was smeared because of her tremors and dementia, just as her wig was on at all angles, but she insisted that I not see her without them. She rambled in her speech, but when most lucid she spoke of the upcoming wedding.

The nights were torturous and I began secretly drinking again, her ravaged form held in my arms in a chair by the bed. Gradually she failed to a point where I could not reach her, but then neither were her pains able to touch her and for this I was thankful.

The night she died I was in a bar. I did not hear of her death until I arrived the next night and found her room empty. I was without hope, even deranged then, permitting the void to gnaw at me without objecting. All my supports had been torn from under me. Returning home from work I would remain half a night at the wheel, sightlessly staring. I randomly toured poor areas on the East side of Dayton, parking my car and sleeping on the seat. All wonder and hope had been vanquished, and I carried on as though entranced. I was ever in the grasp of the void, never sure when the grasp would tighten and even the light of the senses would vanish—rapidly, silently, inexplicably. The void had overwhelmed me, I was not even aware enough to be depressed—it was a neutral state against which the mind was distantly echoing, against which the report of the senses was muted and half noticed.

When months had passed and I had returned to a partial normalcy, I made no attempt to be spiritual or meditate. Nor did I return to the Christian church; I was not even aware for

weeks that I had missed Jill's funeral. Drinking provided the sole hedge I had against the void. More and more I became witlessly drawn into the delirium of bars. As a person I remained dejected and shell-like; but outwardly I was gregarious, so I became more and more popular among the nurses at work, who prior to this had never noticed me. Detached from all spirit, I heedlessly pursued pleasure and risk while engaging in a feast of regret. Even looking at a photograph of the great sage Ramana Maharshi brought a shudder up from my heart, though I would not admit until much later that it was not the spirit that had rejected me; I had insisted on rejecting the heart.

Chapter Eleven

Riding the Current of Death

The void dwells in the body;
death is the precious jewel;
rebirth is the refiner's fire;
If I had been born a goldsmith
there would no need to seek God.

Months passed, and the bouts of mindless wandering ended. I read novels, but no spiritual works. I worked more hours. When I was extremely relaxed there were episodes when I had a sense of being overwhelmed with an unspeakable love and deep purpose. Glimmering in this experience was a rare hope.

That was in 1978, and it was prelude to yet one more death experience. I was spending the night in my parents' upstairs room, a sewing room with a spare bed. That night a most peculiar and intense dream occurred. I dreamed that I got up from bed and peered from the window at a dark car approaching along the road behind the house. The dawn was slanting into the neighboring lawns and from across the sky a jewel-like light was approaching. Then I awoke and went to the window. Gazing at the dawn, I witnessed the exact scene I had just dreamed—except for the light. I was most concerned with the whereabouts of the light, but I returned to my warm bed, stretching out on my back. As soon as I settled under the covers, my attention was drawn to the middle of my head, where light was pulsating. Mesmerized by this fast-flowing light that spun into pinwheels of fire and spread into a mist-like vapor, it seemed as though I was looking at the energy patterns that animated the mind. And I was riding this light as though riding a spirit wind, and it was so wonderful that I was not even concerned when a numbness began settling into my legs.

As the numbness rose through my body there was a sharp pain in each area and then all sensation was gone. Quickly, all sense of even having a body disappeared and all that I remained conscious of was the fire in my head. Below me, approaching from a great depth, was a surf-like roar of energy which swept into me in a thunderous overture. I was drawn along with it, swept up in the energy. I rushed out the top of my head, passing into a heavenly panorama. I ascended among glowing palaces floating in celestial night. Slowing, I arrived in a transparent room where I met a bird-like figure in black robes. She led me around the room and as she did pictures appeared, as though the room was a gallery. The robed figure pointed at each, gesturing as though prompting me to grasp what each was imparting. Though rich and beautifully made, the pictures grew hazy as I strained to examine them. No matter how I strived I could not see the images, as though blinded by them. Even the figure grew indistinct, more presence than image.

Suddenly I was returned to bed, strength seeping back. Making my limbs obey required all of my will. My entire body was an instrument out of tune as I climbed from bed and breathed the sweet morning air at the open window. I was disturbed, for I could recall each detail except for the pictures, which were apparently the axis about which this strange event turned. I had failed to receive whatever message was being offered, a message that according to the figure's manner was most crucial. Yet it depressed me more that I was again having such experiences, experiences that had proven to be such a curse. Soon it dawned upon me that I had been given a message and that it was not a matter that could be translated into mere thought, but was a deeper transmission.

I pored over texts on spiritual practices from the East and found a description of this latest experience of energy in the literature on *shabd yoga*. This description along with my former research into kundalini and in the light of my previous death experiences enabled me to achieve an overview of the entire death process. All that had appeared so convoluted and contradictory assumed a readable pattern.

Shabd yoga is a practice of soul projection from northern India. Its most notable practitioner was the poet Kabir, a Muslim citizen of mediaeval India, though he is famous for his Hindu Guru and many Buddhist influences. He spoke both of the path of Divine Love, or Bhakti, and the North Indian meditation practice of "soul ascent," such as practiced by Parahamsana Yogananda. *Shabd* is defined as a sound or vibration rising out of the void and supporting all existence. According to the saints of the tradition, the experience of Shabd is referred to as "dying while living." The vibration manifests itself as an unstruck melody or light in the spiritual (middle) regions of the head associated with the ajna chakra, or third eye. The light and sound are visible and auditory manifestations of the fine vibration that is the source of kundalini energy. So there were the same lights and sounds I experienced in the practice of kundalini, but I had never meditated exclusively on the vibration.

I began to draw parallels between the processes of kundalini yoga and shabd yoga. To begin with, kundalini energy must be unlocked so that it ascends a course along the spine that can be harsh and turbulent. In shabd the practice is to gently coax the same energy upward by meditating upon the vibrating sound in the middle of the head. In shabd, all the lower chakras are shut down, as in death; in kundalini yoga practice, the lower chakras are permitted to flower and act as a conduit for the energy. Because the process of shabd imitates death, the soul invariably rises from the crown of the head.

Both kundalini and shabd work within the context of a "subtle" or energy body upon which the physical body is dependent to support consciousness. In kundalini we essentially explore the possibilities of our subtle nature. In contrast, shabd is concerned with the subtle body only as a vehicle for ascent into higher realms.

Whereas the point of kundalini yoga is to raise energy and merge it with the formless consciousness (God) that meets with the body at the level of the seventh chakra just above the head, the point of shabd is to provide a gate for the soul to higher realms though the sixth chakra in the middle of the head. In shabd most of the energy remains behind. In kundalini the entire map of energy within the human form is turned inside out and rises into God.

In the rare case when the kundalini is completely aroused, God—or the formless absolute—is immediately attained. This perfect awakening of kundalini is the nirvakalpa samadhi that I experienced with Elaine in 1969. In shabd there is not nearly as much energy behind the ascent because the chakras are not roused, so that soul must rise up and willfully seek this formless God. In shabd, hundreds of such travels may be required to attain the goal, each gradually carrying the soul a little higher, but in nirvakalpa samadhi it is attained in one tremendous leap.

The soul, according to the kundalini yoga tradition, must pass out of a chakra at death; each of these chakras of energy, or vortices as they appeared to me, possesses an energy pattern that either attracts or repels the soul, depending on its merits and tendencies. So we actually tend to live from certain chakras. According to all traditions I have examined, the desired chakra for the soul to depart from at death is the crown chakra, so that the soul is swept upward upon the departing current of energy.

Books on out-of-body experiences normally describe a cord made up of light that connects the soul to the physical body; this cord extends from the naval or heart region, each an abode of a major chakra. It looked to me as though the intensity of the energy flow depended upon which chakra the person projected from. If the energy flow was disconnected, death became irrevocable. Shabd was a more refined process depending upon a higher chakra that usually requires stern practice to accomplish. As Kabir wrote:

> On its own the melody
> resounds in each vessel,
> constantly, without a break,
> the soul and shabd
> have become one,

the mouth is not needed
to repeat the words.[6]

My out-of-body experiences were again set into motion, but the subtle body was not a mirroring of the physical body but a sphere of bright awareness; and by just willing it, I could rise into subtler realms. I recognized the same force or momentum as in my death experiences, except I was capable of exerting my will upon it. Unlike the death process, when we are simply out of body, the mind remains intact and its deep patterns are not unraveled. At death, according to my experience, it is as though the mind is ruptured and its aspects rush out to be gradually reformed, usually resulting in rebirth. Until this juncture I had not looked upon the subtle body as particularly significant.

Hope was slowly being restored, not just in spiritual practice, but in penetrating what was outside the bounds of the physical. I was again gazing into the death process. Disassociation from the physical body was a continual aspect of the kundalini experience, either in sleep or waking, with or without the appearance of a subtle form. Often I just slipped out of the body into states of formless bliss—an almost deathlike swoon. I devalued most out-of-body experiences as occult, rather than spiritual, presuming little about their nature. But this subtle, or energy, body seemingly contained by the physical was suddenly at the heart of my spiritual experiences. This subtle form was like the physical in that it contained mind and will, though its energies were not harnessed according to rigid shapes and laws but flowed with the mind. The subtle body is subject to the mind, instantly responding to its commands. So when I willed it to "rise," the subtle body ascended into more immaterial worlds. When I wanted to return to the physical body I just willed it. No words were needed; the subtle body was so exquisitely sensitive that even a slight intention was enacted. It became apparent that when we are out of body, pure will is not hidden but is our most important aspect.

Practicing out-of-body experiences each night, I eventually arrived at a barrier in the form of utter darkness. Eventually I found the courage to plunge into the darkness and found that the subtle body emits the light that permits its passage across this barrier. Once across, the subtle body merged with pure light.

Interestingly, outside the physical body I was not the same mind as I was within the physical bounds. My responses were frequently surprising and yet neither could I disown them. Perhaps the most curious discovery was that if I engaged the quiet mind when out of body, the experience would abruptly conclude, without any sense of transition. This realization removed all fear of out-of-body journeys, even when I would feel that familiar tug of death, because no matter what I encountered I could shed the entire affair by quieting my mind.

At this juncture I depended upon these journeys to define the spiritual. Even though the death process was laid bare, I did not presume that I was enlightened or that these episodes could necessarily even lead to enlightenment. Frequently I viewed them as no more than entertaining, a way of touring a resplendent and mystical inner space.

My skill with meditation enlarged the range of these experiences. I stumbled upon a technique for inducing out-of-body travel by just plugging my ears prior to going to bed, listening to the harmonious hum and ringing of the shabd until I heard a host of discordant noises and vibrations that marked passage out of the physical body. As soon as I was asleep I was usually out of the physical body.

I remained aloof and detached socially, but retained a host of acquaintances. I was ever spouting humor as I looked upon daily life as no more than a form of creative play. I seemed to disconnect from the physical body even when awake, for lapses in memory would occur from which I would wake to find that I had traveled to an unfamiliar location or was engaged in a task I was not aware of undertaking. I could slip into disengaged internal quiet where I would have dream-like experiences and then wake up to find I had actually been carrying on a conversation. All the turbulence had initiated a metamorphosis, and in retrospect it seemed that I was being prepared for an important event. I existed within a fount of transforming energies, but the confidence I possessed in regard to death seemed to make me less rather than more spiritual. I was by turns elated and slightly depressed, for spiritual life seemed a magic show without a terminal point. Each process that I hoped was leading to enlightenment seemed just a newer, more remarkable magic, and I lacked the maturation or balance that I presumed were necessary for enlightenment.

I began working nights and remaining up nights even when not at work—a habit I have retained. Within the hospital I was rotated among a host of jobs, most of them menial. That winter I applied to nursing school, accepting finally that I belonged in that setting, where the heart of human experience was fully exposed. In our culture, the dying are relegated to a ghostlike existence among sterile wards so that the fragile, perpetually threatened nature of the human condition never has to be examined or meditated upon. Death had led me along my entire life, so it was apparent this was where I belonged. Eventually I would understand that my life was defined by a calling to help individuals in their own approaches to death.

What marked this phase as most unusual to me was that I began taking naps just prior to reporting to work each night. During these naps I remained conscious, though there were no motions, no process of mind within the consciousness—just bare awareness of being aware. This is what is described in the non-dual tradition of Vedanta as *jnana samadhi*, but I did not then describe it so, even though I had read such accounts. It was just a nightly ritual from which I would spring up refreshed and hurry off to work. No person entered the state and none emerged from it; there was just a dropping of selfhood and a resumption afterward.

Without this spiritual practice emerging, I may not have recovered from Jill's death and the disappointments leading up to it. Throughout that period I worked at the hospital and engaged without apology in human pleasures, especially sex, which I had once not permitted myself in an assumption that it would dampen the spiritual flame. I barely related to the person I had been; his history was a lanced wound, and I happily stood apart from him. Hope had been realized in unraveling the puzzle of death, but healing was not to begin until I met a most remarkable woman.

Chapter Twelve

Gift of the Goddess

There is no cure for death.
But birth can be healed.
The Goddess has the balm
on her fingers; quicker
than light she unfurls
each of a thousand petals.
Most gracious though,
is her human form.

Catherine had achieved much with her life and was a person of bright gifts who had never cast aside her spiritual calling. Although she had a degree in English literature, when we met she was studying chemistry. Recently passing a summer at an Indian reservation, she engaged in annual retreat at a Trappist monastery in Arizona. She had a broad, wondering face with eyes that dazzled. She was of Catholic upbringing, a strong resonance of her religion in her nature. Her memories were blessed with saints who materialized and spoke to her, prayers that sank into her heart; if she had been born centuries ago, sainthood would have been her path. Wanting most to be a healer in the ancient sense as a blending of the mind and the heart's wisdom, Catherine's goal was to provide loving care that respected the human being, which was habitually excluded from the hospital climate. Soon she would be attending medical school and was to balance that approach with the approach of the world's shamans and a range of folk remedies: massaging out poisons, brewing herbs, visualizing cures; her practice of sanctioned medicine would be just an element among many.

What was important to me, though, was that with Catherine I was adopted into a spiritual partnership that would heal and rejuvenate me. Catholicism resonated within me as well, for I had harbored visions of Mary and angels even though I was only randomly exposed to the tradition. My heritage was Catholic, but my father had rejected the church and so what religion I knew in growing up I borrowed from his mother. This was a past that I was ashamed even to admit to until I met Catherine. I had not assumed visions to be the fruit of the sane mind, but Catherine was the most sane person I had ever met and through her I began to accept my panorama of spiritual experiences as a grace.

When I first met Catherine, she had just been hired on in the emergency room. A palpable energy profoundly disturbed me, and yet I desperately wanted to speak to her. On the first evening of our meeting, I pursued her into a hallway and found her equally drawn to speak to me. We walked into a vacant meeting room to talk privately, and she sat across the table from me. As soon as we were seated, we were both struck out of body, fully aware that this was a shared event. It was as though our awareness had expanded outward, above and around the physical body, while incredible energies and pressures forcibly pushed down on the larger space we were inhabiting. When we sank back into the physical body, it was as though every imaginable pressure point had been energized. This would become a common experience for us, as though our relationship existed outside the physical realm.

Gradually, and as much as I resisted, Catherine reengaged me in the spiritual. Aware that I was in desperate need of healing, she massaged and bathed me, suggesting a regimen of herbs, providing an energy and spiritual nourishment that I had never met. I had never been quite so intimate with a human being, yet the intimacy did not need the support of sex. Our minds inexplicably overlapped, communicating without speech. The most playful out-of-body experience I ever happened across occurred on a night when I was sharing her bed. That night I slipped out of body and was immediately aware she was with me. We soared side by side in a weightless, ethereal dance—it was an exhilarating experience. And when we slipped back into the body we awoke simultaneously, amazed at what had just transpired.

She remained saintlike in her approach, almost a mediaeval visionary. I was again meditating on pure being, though without a trace of my former zeal. I pursued it casually at first—preferring warmth and pleasure that could be depended upon. But when I meditated upon the quiet mind, there were random occasions when the room overflowed with a gracious presence that transformed all that it touched, touching all points as it flowed. This was a marvel, a form of spiritual lightning that she had renewed, energized—and she provided me with the courage to start over. But I had fully embraced the outer world and was hesitant to sweep it aside.

On an afternoon in the spring of 1979, while we were hiking in the woods, I described to her my meditation on the empty mind which I was again practicing. Sitting beside a stream, Catherine quickly plunged into an interior quiet that was all-consuming. She was adept at the practice in just a week and was soon as wounded by it as I had been, for she had sunk helplessly into the vacuum that I finally realized then to be a stage, a passage, described by St. John in his autobiography as the "dark night of the soul."

As a visionary Catherine had flourished, but this meditation with its deathlike void was just too much to bear. She recoiled from its harshness and in the process was stripped of the sacred that had seemed her birthright, just as I had been. The void, I was learning, required a journey through the death it represented to rebirth in which a painfully acquired wisdom is implicit. The spiritual journey is no mere process of growth as we are led to expect, but a fitful motion that is both death and renewal.

Catherine was in torment, her spirit laid bare beneath the chimera of mind, but when she needed most my recompense for her love I was paralyzed. I was not prepared to be tested again and so did not respond to her pleas. All that was lacking in me was made apparent; Catherine had only herself to depend upon for passage through the dark night.

Just before she left for medical school a strange and moving experience occurred. Late one night, I pulled off the road and opened the side panel of my van, and we huddled there, gazing across a horizon filigreed with trees and night lights. Just above the trees we noticed a speck, a glimmering star or planet, I assumed, until it began leaping about, not as though flooded with wind, but streaking about purposefully. Catherine and I were linked, watching in consonance as the light rapidly grew into a milky white sphere that was astoundingly large. Soon it exchanged its whiteness for a color, then a torrent of colors in rapid succession as though racing across the spectrum. Aware that we were provoking or initiating the experience, we concentrated on it. As though responding, the globe burst apart into a host of perfect geometrical shapes that had seamlessly comprised the shining sphere. The shapes began orbiting around a common point in a dazzling array of pattern and color. It was a mathematician's puzzle made animate, redefining and reshaping itself.

I was then struck with the message, welling up from within, that one of the shapes was preparing to approach us. For a moment we remained fiercely concentrated, then, aware that I was about to be overwhelmed with a tidal wave of light, I began whispering excitedly to Catherine. In response to our lapse in concentration, the shapes immediately ceased moving and were drawn back into their intricate puzzle, the sphere again white. The radiance then contracted until it was just a point of light hopping about as though performing a ritual—and then it vanished.

Years afterward, I finally realized that this display was vitally significant. It was a review of the process of birth and death—

the essential map of all creation. Within the dark space of consciousness there is a flare-up of white light. This white light expands and is refracted and from its rainbow all energy and life appear. These lights are the process of all birth and death, from entire galaxies to the death of a mere moth; the process is displayed and repeated. And it is said in *The Tibetan Book of the Dead* that the white light of creation repeatedly appears to us during death, providing us with a moment's chance of liberation. The bond that Catherine and I shared was founded upon an unimaginable fount of energy, as though we were halves of a spiritual circuit. Catherine represented the spiritual life, and so I was both attracted and repelled by her, just as I both desperately needed and rejected the entire spiritual ordeal. She was the exact reflection of my spiritual tumult, so that I both longed for her and was threatened by her.

Catherine had been repeatedly wounded by my contradictory signals and we grew apart, she again on the course she had set for herself. She soon departed for medical school and though we remained in contact, I never quit disappointing her. When I last heard from her she had started a medical practice in Minnesota, incorporating ancient healing, just as she had envisioned.

Catherine was the Goddess incarnate; the healing she performed still resides deep in my spirit, her imprint eternally upon me. I am indebted to her because without her healing I would not have been able to experience what was to come, the encounter in a convent garden which would change my life.

Part Two

The Ladder in the Heart

Chapter Thirteen

The Priest in the Garden

*There are numberless deaths
and numberless pains;
but just one joy
the soul can reach.
When the flower
of the heart is picked
it blows into the light.*

The night in 1979 when I met Father Thomas it had been drizzling rain at the seminary, rain which froze when it struck the earth, holding onto whatever it touched. The wind was like a cold grindstone and I was seated on the bench beneath the uncompromising figure of Mary in a niche in the stonework of a manmade hill. Conifers provided a somber shade, even at night. Beneath Mary a fountain spilled into a tiny pond edged by stones that were spray-shined in the cold.

I had begun visiting this place in secret at night, and I either sat and gazed vacantly or implored Mary, though for what purpose I was not sure. Once priests had been trained here and monks sang along the march of day into night, but it had gradually lapsed into no more than a country parish, the glory of the monks replaced with buildings in which a religious digest was printed and more buildings which could be rented for seminars. A small number of rooms were kept for the purpose of spiritual retreat.

By day an old monk or nun would roam across the lawn, enhancing its atmosphere. There seemed to be no purpose for the many religious statues that stood dejected in hedges, waded in ponds, or lurked in quiet glades. In the summer, gurus appeared or Zen chanting echoed, their templates of spirit forming and just as quickly dispersing. The land had been acquired from a once-prosperous assembly of Shakers who were, along with the entire Shaker ideal, fading from history. Heedlessly the church razed their remarkable structures. A stone barn in the untended expanse across the road was their sole legacy.

I had loved this place since I met with it. So at night, usually twice or more a week, I would meditate at its grotto, which on this particular night was rigid with winter. Or, not strictly meditating, on many a night I just pondered the experiences that I had had in the cold shade beneath the aspect of the Virgin.

Father Thomas appeared in the door of the rectory, thin against the light, his white beard glowing as he approached. "God cannot be conjured up," he remarked delightedly as he examined me at length. "He is what He is and where He is according to design."

His features were prominent, no doubt made more prominent by his advanced age, and his gaze seemed deep and dim until it met mine, when his eyes flared brightly. In a tattered brown robe he was the animation of an apostle's icon, or an image robbed from a pilgrim's dream. Either way, I knew that he was mine, that this flesh or image belonged to me—that I was suited to its purposes and it mine.

I managed no more than a nod in response.

"Your love, not all your wondering and regret, will lead you back to God. You must look through all those fanciful images you have collected."

"I thought you were a fanciful image," I muttered.

He smiled as though genuinely pleased by my response and

seated himself on the bench, nudging me until he was settled upon three-quarters of it.

"Father Thomas," he introduced himself.

I stammered part of my name and he began speaking.

"The communion of love is ever with us; just trust in it. It is untainted and belongs to God, existing within the same space as God."

"Well," I snorted defiantly, "love can be elusive and almost impossible to define."

"Thought. You are confusing thought with love. Human thought has numberless purposes and serves numberless masters. There are even thoughts which claim to be love, but love is a glory not bound by thought, a design which has no shape or edge. Love must be thoughtless, without seeking order. Thought is often kind, even charitable, but it cannot approach or touch the sacrament of love."

"You speak like a priest."

He frowned, then added, "Only love leads out of hell."

"Well, then it is indeed fortunate that I don't believe in hell," I remarked.

"Don't be deluded by the quickness of thought," he said kindly, though his gaze was more secret and appraising.

"I've spent time there," he spoke again. "Hell is a lightless pit where souls have been cast off, an earthworks where souls worship what is clever, practicing seduction and trickery, but the only hoax they ever bring off is upon their own souls. All that we claim and possess is a weight upon the soul if we are not loving and spending our wealth along love's journey. It is difficult to be set free because thought is quick and random, providing an unsteady surface through which love can't be glimpsed. The brunt of human thought is repetitious and petty, a forest in which love is hiding. If the souls in hell would turn their backs they would find a stair leading upward. Above there is a university where the soul can be reclaimed. I taught there once."

"Taught? When? What are you saying?" My mind was racing. Was he speaking in metaphors?

He shrugged. "It may have been hundreds of years ago."
"In another life," I stammered.

"There is just this life," he smiled, standing up and brushing at the coarse, sharp edge of his robe. "But I am willing to share it."

"I don't understand."

"Of course you don't," he replied, pointing back toward the rectory with his chin. "I'm mad—but then I'm almost ninety—I'm entitled." He chuckled as he strode across the slate court into the light from the door. "Would you like to step in and warm up?"

The scene seemed to have been extracted from a dream that I once had, the light from the door varnishing the path as I regarded this person, whose life's-breath was love. Mad trickster or saint—either case was preposterous, just as was most of his rambling speech. But I was thoroughly enticed and thoroughly in need and so I accompanied him inside. As with all events concerning Father Thomas, even though I have never had a great memory, his heart sermons have stayed with me, sonorous and intense.

The rooms within the priory were plain, bluntly Christian, hung with Madonnas and quotes from scripture. A plaster Jesus with his heart outside his cloak stood on a wooden table. The priest switched on a lamp with a patched shade and motioned me to sit across from him in the dim light, as though we were about to engage in a seance.

"The soul makes our images," said Father Thomas, patiently regarding me. "Images are near to the soul, whereas the usual ragtag of thought is on the edge, requiring a great journey to move from quiet mind into the soul. For the mind is quieted by suppressing thought, so it is from the province of thought that we are starting off. Whereas our soul is near to our dreams. Even a misshapen dream or dream image is much nearer the soul than a perfect philosophy.

"The more precious and bright an image seems, the more of the soul nature it partakes in. Our most intense dreams carry the soul's imprint, speaking to us from what we have named 'our hearts.' And all that a vision is is an image that is full of the soul's energy. What makes it so compelling is not what it portrays, but the energy it translates. The true outflow of the soul, though, the true nature of the soul, is love."

"Wait, wait," I said. "I am confused. What is this all about?"

"I'm helping you," said Father Thomas, looking rather perplexed by my outburst.

"Helping me? You are confusing me."

"What part of it is confusing you?"

I sighed impatiently, more impatient with myself than him, for I was at a loss to explain my anger.

"Listen," said Father Thomas sternly, "I am providing help. I think that you need help."

"Yes. Yes," I agreed with him, and then myself. "But I don't understand, this soul, these images."

"You did ask me to explain love."

"Yes, I don't understand that either."

"Yes, that's true," said Father Thomas. "If I explain the soul it is reduced to fragments and pieces." But quickly, running it into these words, he launched into an explanation. "The soul is perpetual motion, an overwhelming brightness from the spirit pours out, animating all the worlds, the world's minds, all that is exists. From these energies a mind is conjugated.

"If we are practiced enough to quiet the mind we are not in the soul or God, but just pushing against the energies pouring out of the spiritual into the personal, so that we are hiding both our minds and our souls in the process. Which is unfortunate, for it is this outpouring of spiritual riches that is the love we are seeking; God's light passes through the soul, through a pattern there, and dreams are made, from these dreams the mind springs up. If we choose the light that pours out of the soul over the images or the dreams, then we have found God. God is in that outpouring, that grace, that flood that we can speak of as energy or a holy spirit. Or we can speak of it just as God, for it is God that is shining through all-souls."

"That is more explanation than I expected," I confessed.

Father Thomas tugged at his beard, as though judging what he had just said. "Or so I think. What is required is that we are transparent to God, that we are neither empty before him nor become an opaque fount of energies; we must be open. If we are transparent then we intuit God's Light against a primal stuff, energies, against the trappings of the mind and a roar of images, but God remains apparent not because we have found him but just because we are open, receptive. Our souls are molds that God pours through and by which God makes the world, all worlds."

"God makes a world through our images?"

"Yes, yes, we dream it up. You, me, the wall of this room, we dream it up. We are born into our dreams; we never tire of it, it seems."

"Reincarnated."

"No," laughed the priest, "we are just chasing our dreams." Father Thomas looked upon me with a puzzled disquiet, but his patience had not been exhausted.

"Let me suggest a practice," Father Thomas finally said, leaning back in his chair. "Each person is a story, or a work of dreams. This story is what we are born to—it is our reason for being. The images can be life-shaping or just an ordinary story we particularly like, or a sense of magic that is accompanied by no distinct image, a deep-seated intuition, but it must possess a purity and innocence that we depend upon most. These dreams and dream images underpin all that we do and say; if we are reborn then it is because we are not yet done composing the stories we hold dear."

Strangely, all that he had explained seemed to be a part of me, as though he were touching upon what was most dear and precious to me. It was as though I had been poised, preparing to hear him speak since birth. Even his voice seemed to resonate within me, as though even the breath was part of an invaluable secret.

It was past four in the morning and Father Thomas went to the kitchen to brew coffee. I drank a single cup of very strong coffee and Father Thomas was silent for more than an hour. I leaned against my chair, a joy as firm as a bone in my heart, not my imagined heart, but my physical heart. And from my physical heart it was being pumped throughout my body.

Suddenly, Father Thomas tilted back in his chair, his chair legs gripping the patched rug beneath the table, and from beneath closed eyes he began to speak. "You must just learn to relax and permit an image to leap to mind, permitting the strong river of your imagination to flow; for it is that flow that we most depend upon. What we refer to as mind is not originating within us, but passing through us as a current that we cannot see except as pure motion and as the dreams it kindles. As we rest amid the images we must learn to permit the current to dictate and flow along with it.

"What is important is that it is made pleasant, that we enjoy the practice as a play, a numinous glory brimming through our imagination. What is most crucial though is that we do not attempt to look at or catch this flow; we must just remain in contact with it, touching the flow rather than looking at images. When we have learned to touch our imagination rather than look at it, we are overwhelmed with pure energies—we are embraced with the rapturous outpourings of love. It is more simple than you think," he added quickly.

Light was glancing from the roof and the forest south of the seminary proper had begun to breathe and chant over the morning when I stood and departed, Father Thomas sagging in his chair asleep. I hurried, almost ran, toward my car, for if this meeting with Father Thomas had been providential, it had been just as overwhelming and disturbing.

For weeks I was tormented with thoughts of the hell Father Thomas had described, pondering as well the university above it where the kind Father supposedly lectured the damned. This was the message that I had most potently received; all thoughts of soul and the soul's light and the soul's images were tumbling as though in a blinding wind, but the picture of hell that was slowly developing in my head was mesmerizing. I even imagined that Father Thomas was the last of his kind and those imprisoned there were obliged to await his return. It seemed conceivable that the souls in hell have no concept of freedom; or perhaps they preferred it there and did not wish for an intercession in their behalf. Perhaps—and this seemed plausible to me—those imprisoned in hell found the university to be invisible. I envisioned that those in hell could sense it, but because they were literally blind to it just could not find it.

Finally one morning the most disturbing of all possibilities occurred to me. Perhaps I was in hell and had just located the priest and the university, most of which remained elusive to me. This planet I lived upon could be described as an earthworks and the pursuits of the common man have much in common with those imprisoned in hell.

For several days I chose not to visit the priest, adrift as I was in my own thoughts. Nor had I practiced as he had suggested. When I finally returned to my night perch beneath the serene gaze of the Virgin, he was not shaken out of the seminary as I expected. There was a ferocious wind sweeping beneath the pines that night and eventually I huddled in my coat, assuming a quiet regular breathing, and attempted to form an image of the Virgin in my mind. An image that should have been emblazoned on my retinas would not appear intact—all those nights I was bending under her gaze and I could not make her appear; it seemed as though she insisted on mixing with patterns, pictures, stories that the mind was playing out, though the scenes were hazy, running over with ephemeral shapes and figures partially drawn. The imagination was not as I had imagined it; there was not as much fantasy as just untraceable motion—an uncharted sea. But then I realized that was the point of it; I gave up materializing a Virgin and just kept in touch with that motion. Quickly my body was a rushing of energies and the familiar blue seed leaped out of me, shining brightly and wonderfully, and a surge of energy climbed my spine, culminating with a great pleasure in my head. This was repeated again and again until I was both exhilarated and exhausted. It was unmistakable that I had been cleansed in a pure fountain of kundalini.

I returned home, deciding that I would embark upon a fast and tune my habits to this energy, repeating my late night vigils until the priest reappeared or I found the courage to approach him. I returned home that night elated from the energy but disappointed I had not met with Father Thomas.

Chapter Fourteen

To Be Mad and Loving

*When the mind is lush with fire
and slain with love; the stone
of the spirit made weightless—
until just God remains.*

That same winter I decided to drop out of the nursing program and applied for admittance in the respiratory therapy program, taking preliminary courses and rooming at my parents' so that I could scrape together tuition money. I had picked up a book on haiku in a discount bin at the college bookstore. I was enchanted with these plain, natural epigrams and began composing them. I had not written in a while, but the haiku were to me accessible and strong, which was all that I required of a poem. I had no excuse for not practicing as Father Thomas had instructed me, but over the winter I was more intent on experimenting with haiku and ink prints.

Not until an unusual dawn visit that next spring did Father Thomas again approach me—or, more accurately, did I stumble across him. He was at a modest garden that I had seen a pair of nuns tending. Plush with ripening vegetables and herbs, it was protected with a barrier of mesh. Dressed in a pair of tattered overalls, the priest labored with pliers on this barrier. I just watched, not speaking, expecting that Father Thomas was making a repair. Only slowly did it dawn upon me that he was not exacting a repair but inflicting an injury that I calculated would be sufficient to admit a rabbit. As he ended his work, he smiled up at me, as though pleased with the task he had undertaken.

"I wondered when you would see me again." His smile lengthened as he tucked his pliers into the back of his faded trousers.

"I have looked for you, expecting that you would find me," I confessed, "but did not have the courage to knock on your door."

"No," he sniffed, looking up as though gauging the weather, "you just did not see me."

"That doesn't make sense," I replied rather defiantly.

"Don't worry, don't worry," the Father replied. "Once you give up the habit the adjustment is rather minor."

"What habit?"

"Not using the mind as God intended. You have not practiced as we discussed?"

"I have, but there are many projects that I have taken on."

"Look," he shrugged pleasantly, "I am a Christian, God forbid. A Christian and therefore I speak like a Christian. And projects just pass by; we are buried beneath our projects, markers claiming we belonged to such and such and were born on this day and died on this one. I am a Christian and according to my creed God is love, and that's all that's worth minding.

"To be transparent to God," he continued, "is to mend a spirit tattered by competition and greed. We are a crew on a sinking ship. There are no shores and no edges to this experience that we are presently having—and so there is no safe harbor. We all die. Yet all that we are consumed with is achieving rank, improving our looks, and having more than our neighbor."

More frail and human in appearance, perhaps too human, the priest coughed and muttered through his speech. Even his gaze was spare and penetrating, as though his acquaintance with death was more than casual.

"There are many sacred paths to God, but what they all depend upon is a breakthrough, a piercing of the heart that reveals a divine love that was invisible and is now omnipresent. We are compelled to love because we are all immersed in God and He has been brought from what seemed a great distance into the present. The content or nature of the breakthrough is not so important; what is crucial is that we have met with God.

"We must separate our soul from the meshes of pride and greed. When the mind is transparent then we are harmonized with experience, whereas the usual mind is a practice in discordance.

"Love is raging within us and it must not be cooled; the flames must be fanned. When we love, God shines through us with such force that we burn up. I talk too much," he added, searching for his pliers. "Too much, too much," he admonished himself, turning abruptly and heading away from me.

"Enough," he called back. "If we meet again we must talk this over. Too much and too little has been said."

As I might have expected, he was angered at my lack of progress. When I was far from him he just seemed an addled priest coaxing me along his path and seeking to mend me with fables of Christian love. He wanted me to imagine so profoundly that God is engendered; we cease seeking to be loved through all the objects in the world and are loved because God shines through us; then we are infinitely loved and loving, which are not separate or separable. It was all so plain, an odyssey of the heart and spirit that was all that mattered. But when I was away from him it all faded, even his gift for looking into me. It was all less than unique, swept and explained away. It was as though when he was not present the temporal and personal overwhelmed as never before, perhaps because his spirituality was too genuine for me to grasp.

Because of Father Thomas, though, I was more interested in the Christian religion, which I had never looked into except in most desperate need. I attended a host of meetings and services, though I preferred the Pentecostal, Greek Orthodox, or Catholic, for each was possessed of its own particular energy. It seemed as though my spiritual sensibilities were being renewed and awakened. I was most at home among Charismatic Catholics, a group that rejoiced and danced with spiritual energies in a manner similar to the Pentecostals, though along with the energy they possessed the treasures of their own saints and contemplatives.

When I practiced as Father Thomas encouraged, I just conjured up an image and permitted it to flow away—beneath it would be an infinite inner space. The raising of kundalini was replaced with this shapeless, unbounded inner space. There were the inner lights and sounds of kundalini and beneath that a lightless and soundless space, the same as pure being except that it was not a mere silence, but a radiant depth of being. And I saw, too, that each person's story was composed of the riches of imagination and constellations of energy which were the outgrowth of an intensity that was an inner infinity. When there is no symbol standing for a self there is no self, there is just God. And all my spiritual seeking and the spiritual lore that I had accumulated was just more imagery of a personhood that made the soul appear dark and opaque.

That summer was luminous and has shined within me ever since. Many secrets were turned inside out and my once-famished life became full and artfully recreated. First, just a week later it dawned upon me that if I wanted to visit Father Thomas and not wait the length of a winter, I should just trust and expect—that the space between visits existed because I lacked these qualities.

So on the occasion of my next visit I trusted utterly in the mad priest and trusted he would be prepared to share a brief walk. And after a fashion I could loosen my bones, settled and stiff from a sudden departure into too much meditation, while picking up what kernels of wisdom or madness Father Thomas was willing to toss out.

Behind a huddle of brick buildings, once a rectory, and opposite a clotted pond was a broad path of pebbles lending itself to a tour of the woodland settled on the eastern-most slope of the property. With patient expectation I stood at the breaking of the path, contemplating maples wrestling with a breeze springing up fresh and pleasant from the direction of the chapel. A breeze that Father Thomas arrived on, leaning into his steps more gingerly than I would have assumed possible. Full milkish beard and spare pink flesh seemingly thrown across his bones, Father Thomas seemed to glow in the day's brilliance, more an apparition and blessing to me than the angel that visited me as a child.

The night before, I had attended a charismatic gathering in the chapel of a parish in town, witnessing nuns no more than dark wisps leap about in trances. And to my surprise a hunched, frail nun who had at first struck me as enfeebled swung about and about as though a dervish dancing with an invisible image until she levitated, inches then more inches, for moments, then more moments, as the frenzied dance continued, until she gracefully reunited with the earth and hobbled away. Nobody noticed, or nobody mentioned it, so I kept it to myself as well. But it was more of a miracle than I had ever experienced in an ashram or zendo.

"Miracles are poison, my boy," commented Father Thomas as he began leading the way across smooth pebbles and leaf mold.

I kept after him, adjusting my pace to his, keeping him aside and slightly ahead.

"If you find that you begin to experience miracles, or rather miracles begin to experience you, then you need to work harder. Your will is weak."

"With all respect, Father, that makes no sense to me."

"To begin with," said Father Thomas, choosing the northern leg of the path, "a man or woman cannot perform a miracle. They can be invited, but miracles perform themselves. They possess you, you do not possess them; therefore they are a danger."

The path grew thin, ancient trees touching and breathing

upon us. Father Thomas did not speak again until we were hiking a downward slope which spread out upon a marsh.

"People look within," sighed Father Thomas, examining his ragged loafers at the frayed edges of his trousers, evidence, I surmised, that he had hiked through this woods as a matter of habit. As I pondered I realized that I had missed a link in Father Thomas's wisdom.

"Eventually they find interior silence, or become self-absorbed. Visions may appear—it is to be expected, as is the random miracle. All to be expected. But what is the purpose? It is all just an instant, a meeting, silence and light, flesh and thought, in God's love. A love that can't truly be examined or penetrated because all else depends upon it.

"And if we dwell in the fullness of this dependency, wherever one steps he will find the paths of heaven. But without love all of existence can be turned upside down and inside out and not a single occasion for rejoicing will be found. Because we shun love, then what shouldn't exist becomes possible and what should exist is made impossible."

Father Thomas sighed and seated himself on a stone that grew up from the edge of the marsh. "Even before the grace and mystery of God gave birth to the awareness—that all-important awareness through which we are led to heaven or hell, learn to separate the light from dark, and track a saviour to a crust of bread or into a psalm—there is love, connecting all that was with all that will be.

"Searching for or figuring out love is a futile exercise. Just be aware and overwhelmed with love, which is a mystery. Love that mystery of God and all that springs from the mystery and recedes into it. There is no summation of God, nor is it possible to explain creation—mystery within mystery is a formless sea over which we must navigate back to God. If we use a compass then we will become hopelessly lost; we must just accept the mystery as our guide to make that passage. All tombs are empty and all rituals must remain an imperfect representation of that mystery."

His words pierced me and I trembled.

"But how is that done?" I whispered, still trembling.

"Be mindlessly overwhelmed with love, rejoicing in and embracing all as though it were a gift—even the gift of suffering. Be transformed by what you love and in loving rest in the divine mystery."

With that Father Thomas rose, a warm haziness at his edges as he adjusted his posture. And then at a quick pace he ascended the hill.

In a breathless rush he spoke again. "Sainthood is a curse; don't seek to be perfect. Perfection is dull and repetitious. Death is all that is perfect—the sort of death that is without sensation or light. To be among the living is to be unpredictably tossed about among the most holy and unholy of possibilities, enchanted, loved, disappointed, sickened and wounded—which is the purpose of birth, to embrace an entire world, not a mute corner to worship. Besides, death and perfection just don't exist; we spring up again and again among possibilities—such is the nature of love's strivings.

"Be a character," he fairly shouted as we plunged back into the hugging woods, "both mad and loving, and therefore maddening to those who insist on being thoughtful and judging. Such people are full of mumbling, competing voices that fill them with confusion."

The path widened, groping as it did among conifers thick and pleasant to the senses. And Father Thomas remained quiet as though permitting me this pleasure.

"Love and become sublimely remade until all your meetings are seen as but a moment that is exceedingly frail and sacred. We are just these frail moments; we have no place to rest our heads except upon them. Love and reclaim the seed that Jesus threw out into the desert, a seed that grew up into a tree of such stature that it is overshadowing all of civilization, even though few have chosen to rest in its shade."

The path spread out and was absorbed in the hull of a gutted structure, its charred floors tracing vanished rooms, its partial walls providing support for their illusion. Father Thomas leaned against a collapsed beam and smiled. Beer cans were strewn all about him.

"Ceremonies were performed on this land by its natives, a tribe that saw with their hearts. Then Shakers danced and sang here, in their trance-like ceremonies seeking transport and grace. Monks have marked it since with vigils, addressing God with their simple, flowing wisdom. But now, now it is an altar for pagan rituals," he laughed as he spread out his arms as though to embrace the evidence of trespassers. "Oh, but we must hurry."

He was right. The night was seeping up from beneath the trees, even though we had begun our walk in the morning and it seemed as though no more than a hour had vanished. The path splintered just past the ruins into a maze of thin, fading tracks. Choosing the offshoot of the path, Father Thomas ducked beneath and scuttled out from under the grasp of the forest, emerging a stone's throw from where I parked. A shadow through the slow summer twilight, Father Thomas made his way back toward a chapel haloed by a weekday evening mass.

The next days, approaching my thirtieth birthday, poured out revelations. What was most apparent was that Father Thomas was not just lecturing, he was communicating with spirit energy. There was a sweet, almost sensuous burning in the regions of my heart, a flame that spread out and passed up along a host of paths into my head. There was a path, as Ramana Maharshi had described, along the right side of the heart, and there was a projection back to the spine, and a halo of perceived energy just beneath the sternum. There were currents of deep pleasure that were constantly being referred to and trance-like submersions in this energy in which I just lay upon the couch and reveled in the sheer pleasure. It was similar in nature to the shakti, or energy of kundalini, but it was much purer, richer, more abiding, and wonderfully overwhelming. This state continued for more than a week, though I began to sense in me a resistance to this pure pleasure. As a result I began experiencing calamities of the physical heart, such as prolonged arrhythmia and palpitations and even episodes in which the heart's rhythm was suspended for many seconds. So in turn I was stretched upon the couch clutching my chest. I experienced a rash on my chest that has continued to reappear to this day and the lymph nodes under my arms would frequently swell.

I had never been prone to what is referred to as *kriyas* in the kundalini journals, which are surging transmissions of power, making the body contort or jump. But when I was in bed, just after I reached into my exhaustion, there would be a surge of energy the purpose of which seemed to throw me from bed; it was not a located force, but rather it seemed as though the entire body was seized with a force that rushed from the extremities inward, so that the limbs were jolted up and aside with such vigor that it almost capsized me from bed. This was not just the energy of kundalini, but was an unbroken spiritual force that did not depend on paths in the body, or chakras, that did not even flow, but descended upon me in a great unbroken wave.

Just so, the energy was not flowing from me as it once had; rather, it just leaped out. It was as though the whole body was being opened through the heart and so there was no more design or map to it than this; body and heart were seized and overwhelmed. It was soon apparent to me that the purpose of shakti was to unbind consciousness, not to perpetuate energies, and that there would be no consummation to this process unless the spirit of love was permitted its freedom. But at this juncture I had no clue as to what that might involve.

Miracles did occur and it was apparent, just as Father Thomas described, but did not pertain to me; rather it seemed more that they were a result of a confluence of events and energies and purposes. There was a night when a nurse was explaining to me the nature of truth according to the gospel, for I had been to church with her, but I was suddenly enraged with her presumption and stood up, asking her where in this room truth was hiding. Instantly I was thrown out of my body and was examining the room from above. The episode was over quickly, but I was aware as it was happening that the woman I was speaking with was having the exact same experience. We were sharing an out-of-body perspective of the room and the long table in the room where our physical bodies were seated. She stumbled out of the room and never preached to me again, except to urge me to appeal to God to rid me of the Devil's power. In an instance when I became angered while at a restaurant, the orb light over where I was seated spectacularly blew up. But I had no sense of the energy of these and other experiences like them; there was just an eruption of force.

I was made aware of the intimate link between breath and energy and the mind; almost always, the breath was attuned to and essentially the same as the inner pulsation of energy. This energy urged images from the depth of mind in a natural rhythm that controlled the mind. This arose from an inner infinity, which, it seemed, I was eternally abiding in whether I was given at that moment to noticing it or not.

I was not deluded into assuming that I had achieved what I had been seeking through Father Thomas's instruction. It was apparent that I was not unconditionally, or even conditionally, loving and temperate in my heart and moods. I had, among the habits acquired in the past decade, become indulgent and vain; and so I was far from tranquil and was just as dedicated to a search for pleasure, as the search for pleasure and the search for experiences through this energy were of exactly the same nature. Either was an outlet for the overriding pressures this energy induced in the physical body. The more the energy matured, the more dangerous it became as it demanded an outlet, regardless of through which chakra it emerged. The energy demanded access; it radiated freely into all the chakras and the related physical organs, seeking either spiritual or temporal pleasure, but always pleasure. The purpose of the energy was to stimulate and engage, to push into and open up, and it did not seem to matter which course was taken.

So it was apparent that I needed to become consciously responsible for the energy. But I had yet to engage Father

Thomas's principal communication that this energy cannot be suppressed or harnessed and the only appropriate channel for it is love. It was his conviction that if the energy is divorced from love, even if a person is apparently enlightened and can perform spiritual feats, the person's state of mind will rise and fall with the natural flow of the energy mindlessly expressed. Love is all that can harness these wild energies and give them sustained form.

Once I began to accept Father Thomas's message, that love was the foundation of all spiritual practices and events, I began to look upon the experiences not as spiritual sustenance or treasure, but as a sign that I was refusing to be transformed. This was the reason that I had had to succumb to so many unusual processes and experiences. I learned that it is not experience that is enlightening, but the wisdom we gain from it. Experiences provide material from which to forge either wisdom or deception. Ordeals occur when we refuse to be transformed by the spiritual practice we have undertaken; such had occurred with me and the dark night of the soul. My resistance to this void had perpetuated its hold upon me. Father Thomas had been required to awaken the infinity that was clenched beneath the void by the harshness of my approach. Yet I would, over the years, continue to resist the transformation that Father Thomas had initiated. Even at this point I had begun to realize that what is most spiritual and precious cannot be grasped. Slowly, inexorably, I began to release my hold on my spiritual experiences—which is the sole road to awakening.

Chapter Fifteen

Becoming Visible to God

> *Seeking refuge between the gates*
> *of the heart, Jesus and Shiva*
> *dancing where there is no form;*
> *just as love has buried*
> *all of God's prophets.*
> *A single pearl on my tongue*
> *even in dreams I'm touched*
> *by this hot coal.*

Twice the next week I went to the seminary seeking Father Thomas and on both occasions was disappointed, yet just a week afterward Father Thomas approached me in the yard in the middle of morning.

I had been transferred back to evening shift at the hospital and was about earlier than usual, wandering the church lawns without direction or purpose. Perhaps I should have just roused the courage to inquire at the door, requesting to speak to the retired priest. I was sufficiently versed in church affairs to realize that if I had inquired I would have been sent in every direction except toward the priest. Perhaps, according to church decree, faith was to remain a labyrinth. I had not yet made amends with the Christian church for Jill's death, which explained both my reluctance to appear at the door and my late night appearances in the outer yard, never once broaching the chapel. But it seemed as though our meetings that summer were part of a design, though I knew not of what nature. So I trusted in that. And I waited in the grotto.

From a distance, I was familiar with the posture and measure of the steps more than the figure itself. And as he grew nearer I wondered if I was mistaken, for this was either not the same person or he had remarkably changed. Drawing near to me, he sat down on the bench we usually shared. He was strikingly thin, as though he had almost worn through in just the past few days. His gaze flickered; his flesh looked as fragile as ancient parchment.

I had heard it said that luminous souls can age backward to forward, even dying before they are born and thereby are born into wisdom, the bottoms of their feet having shaped their path even before they are able to take a step. It sounds much like a Sufi tale. Perhaps it would later be connected to the fables regarding Father Thomas, though I am not able to put it in that context either. Yet it was in my mind precisely as he arrived that perhaps Father Thomas was aging backward to forward according to a design. The thought no doubt just reflected my reluctance to accept that he was ill.

His breath rushed away from him when he spoke. "I have missed you, my friend."

"Have you been unwell, Father?" I asked, taking his hand, a familiarity I had never presumed.

He cupped my hands between his. "Life is a disease, God is the cure," he laughed. "What we refer to as life is a dance upon the head of a pin. Each moment is just as precarious; we just don't notice until we are ill."

"Father, when I meet with you my mind is wonderfully pure; all that once seemed so esoteric and hidden is so simple and evident. I am inspired to love, not because I am seeking or praising God, but just because a force has opened my mind and love flows through. But when we are apart I am again rude and pleasure seeking."

"Our roots have become entwined, we are sharing an imagination and spirit; you are being imprinted with what I have imagined. But then most of your hours are spent with people who imprint you with their story. When you set step from my hermitage you are immersed in the world's dream. You grow opaque to God, and then transparent to Him when you return to me, again dreaming at my side.

"But you are much too attracted to becoming perfect; you haven't decided whether you prefer the Father-God or a God that is the heart's rapture. When we are too given to discussion upon this subject it just becomes a spiritual gossip, a pleasant repast. The world is already subjected to too much seeking of perfection; put that aside and just love. We are not in need of any more shrewd or profound people; what is needed are people who just plainly love without regarding this as special.

"You must inquire again and again of yourself, 'What am I doing at present? Is what I am doing transparent to the Divine or am I opaque and full of the world's dreams? Am I full of purpose, or am I resting upon a love which is without purpose except to love?' It is work, requiring a good deal of self-reflection and practice. Or you can turn it into prayer: 'Lord, make me transparent to the Divine instead of opaque and full of the world's dreams. Take away all purpose so that I may rest in the love that is its only purpose.'"

The priest adjusted his back with a wince and drew an ancient Roman coin from his shirt, or so it appeared, rubbing its image between his tangled fingers. And as he continued he found it more and more difficult to draw his breath back after he spoke, and he paused frequently.

"To love is to be present without distance. When there is pretense, when we are acting according to a plan or expectation, then love must be set aside. For pretense begins with separation, separation that makes love impossible. To be separate is to be stifled, while to love is to be ever overflowing. If love is not at this exact instant flowing freely, then it is just a pretense, or a game. It is not important whether or not we loved in moments past. All that matters is that we are fully and *presently* loving."

For a while the Father gathered his breath. The birds chattered brightly in the trees above us, comforting me, perhaps comforting themselves; then, as though an invisible signal had been given, they were at once silent—a silence that was anchored to the earth by the laboring hum of bees. Above us a breeze in the trees lifted and settled.

"Most people claiming to be spiritual have no love issuing from them. When they speak of the spiritual they are seeking

mystical experiences and promises. Perhaps they want to be saints, perhaps magicians, perhaps they just want wealth and progeny; but it is all the same loveless repetition and need. Whether we are seeking a vision of God or reserving a seat in heaven is of little importance. And to accomplish their goals, many perform rituals and repeat sacred formulas. Yet visions and rituals do not make us visible to God; we become visible by sharing in His nature. And God's nature is a mystery that overflows.

"People crave what makes them weak or sick or mad because their dreams are polluted, all the light in them extinguished. Their minds have been racing since they were children and they have been racing after them. The solution to all this is just to overflow with love, not to pursue dreams that bind us and quell our inner light. We must choose God's dream instead of our own. Then love becomes a force that seizes our hearts and minds."

"Yes, yes," I mumbled, a light passing over my mind exactly as he spoke, a light of such intensity and so absolutely engulfing that I searched about me for its source. It was as though a much brighter sun than the one we know had passed over me.

"You must excuse me," he said. "I have been slightly ill of late." He rose and departed with a stooped, halting gait. His expression was written deeply into his face, his jaw seemed more prominent, and his beard did not seem that same pure white it had a week earlier. And again I fretted that this was not the same man; but this was impossible, for the conversation had been a continuation of all that we had shared.

A last glance followed him through the mid-morning haze stretched upon the freshly mowed lawn. I bowed to the Virgin and departed on the opposite path.

This visit had made me afraid, afraid that the brightness with which he had infused my mind would vanish. I suspected that it was not a matter of a mere transference of wisdom, that the mercury of the priest's energies and the present carnival of my practice would have to, eventually, be reconciled, learned, and ingested. I was having experiences that were remarkable but not experiences which I could comprehend. The kundalini-shakti was not a magic imposed upon the world from the outside; it was a natural world-engulfing magic, a birthright of our species. So it could not just be expected to perform and empower; it was here to be endured and sustained and encouraged until a spiritual being emerged from its radiant womb. The purity that these forces sought was not that of a saint's disgust with human appetites, but a consistent, even blind and unappraising, recourse to love. I was aware that it was important to appreciate that the magic of the kundalini was neither personal nor unnatural, but the inherent glow which is the root of life itself. We have so invested the spiritual with symbols and rituals that it seems distant and unapproachable. But what is required is not saintliness or a purification, but a mere human being who is willing to be tested and transformed according to love's dictates. We must surrender, because surrender is the nature of love. Not a surrender within a framework of belief and ritual, but a surrender that is endlessly performed.

Love appeared to be the binding force, for when the kundalini was tempered with love, the energy harbored a completeness, a force that did not possess separate elements but was consummately loving and generous. Until then the shakti had never appeared to me as a divine blessing.

I began, increasingly, to experience "transports" of the heart, so that the world's pain was a tacit, ever-engulfing reality. The outpouring of energies, then, seemed to arise not so much from a mere opening, but from a wound in the heart made by all the passionate suffering that comprised the world. I became more and more irrationally loving and more and more unpredictable, for love might depend upon me appearing to be a fool to set a person at ease, or wise in order to comfort them. There was no rule or aspect regarding love. The energy was intoxicating as I breathed from the heart, the heart swelling with the inbreath, showering energy with the outbreath. I had been made a part of Father Thomas's life. It was almost as though my body was a house of spirits that we shared.

As though I was being burned up by these energies that Father Thomas had unleashed, I grew thin, though I was not fasting. My weight, which had held at 175 for the past year, was plummeting to barely 150, which upon my six-foot frame was nearly skeletal. I was even thinner than when I had returned from California. I was moving about in this fragile quiet upon which it seemed the influx of raw energy depended, so I avoided casual speech and contact. The priest's love seemed to provide all the human exchange I required. Perhaps my body was accepting Father Thomas's physical imprint along with the flow of his energies.

My exposure to the priest had invoked an exchange of mind and spirit, but what he had most importantly passed on was a tale that was not inside of him, but that he was inside of—a story Father Thomas breathed into and animated with his overpowering will to love. I had not deeply considered the entire story, but I sensed its eternal design and its consummate purposes, for through such a tale a mere person was apparently translated into spirit.

I hesitated to share with anyone the tale I had embarked upon with Father Thomas, for I feared that if our secret was penetrated, much of the potency of the dream would be lost. During most visits to the seminary I never encountered Father Thomas, but was content in sharing the invisible continuum he represented when I just hiked the woods, read on the lawns, or sat in wonder beneath the orbiting night to gaze on the statue of the Virgin. And there was an inherent holiness to this land that touched the innermost part of me—the priest and I had adopted a spiritual history that was inconceivably ancient. There were evenings in particular when this history seemed to reach across the ruins of numberless memories and embrace and consume me.

From the ground up, this land was a conspicuous blessing. Was it the priest's pious, loving heart that had lit the fire within me or was it the land itself? Or had he inherited the torch of the land and passed it on? This humble priest, it seemed, was the midwife of my spiritual birth, but the land was the sacred Mother of which the image of the Mother of God in the grotto was just an obvious, ever-functioning aspect. This image of the Virgin possessed an almost palpable energy—so much so that even on nights before my meeting with Father Thomas, I supposed I had witnessed the statue gesturing or speaking. The statue had drawn me to the grotto, but the priest had been required to provide it with a tangible form.

So in the late months of summer I was content to sit with, to gaze upon, to keep the company of the statue when the priest was not about, for, strange as it seemed, they seemed to be aspects of the same effulgent love. I sat on a bench in the slate yard and adored the Virgin rather than formally meditating, which was just to sit with the circuit of the kundalini opened and pouring out from the heart. And the more I poured out the more I was flooded; the light communicated back and forth between the invisible sun in my heart and the inner infinity of the head, back and forth between my open heart and the representation of the Virgin Goddess. Such a wonder is impossible to express, though perhaps requisite for making the real journey into the radiance of love.

Chapter Sixteen

A Breath in God's Wind

*The lesson of fire
beneath God's silent
mask; the journey
speaking in the bone;
our breath in
the sail of our spirits,
the ocean a blinding light.*

In the fall of 1980 I was slated to begin classes in respiratory therapy at Sinclair College. Pressure was mounting in regard to what to expect from the courses, for though the science was light and the aspects of medicine quite practical and approachable, I had no roots in science. But, even more, I was worried about being expected to perform; except as a painter performance had never been expected of me. I was a person who had a corrosive effect on patterns and expectations. Exchanging my wilderness of meditation for rigid courses and exams, pouring over lecture notes and books—this is what I dreaded. Except as my needs had dictated in the realm of meditation and religion, I had not been a person to engage in study.

Even though I had been repeatedly baptized in holy fire, I had not been inoculated against a round of desires and regressions. As the date approached for class to begin I was more and more preoccupied, standing outside my meditation.

Wisdom is born when spiritual work is expressed through what is temporal and ordinary. Without the ordinary to rest upon, love's wisdom cannot be born. But it was repeatedly my mistake to reject this foundation of spiritual work. When I was apart from Father Thomas I tended to reject "mere love," taking the rarified phenomena that spiritual work conjured as its purpose. Late that fall, when there was a lull in the appearance of spiritual signs and energies, I quit making my almost nightly visits to the seminary. Once outside the sacred ring of that land and without contact with a sacred figure, the meditation of the heart rapidly evaporated and I was quickly dependent on the trappings of the social and personal. I had not managed to translate the love that Father Thomas had rhapsodized upon into an endurable, human context, and so when human exchange was demanded love was set aside. It was soon apparent that the summer of inner feasts was over—that it had been a passing spectacle. That is how I looked at it then, not relating it to my lack of wisdom and resolve.

Soon I was possessed by a flurry of dreams—play-like dreams awash in grief and regret. Dreams that, once hatched, refused to retreat into the quicksand of the unconscious, but remained with me as fitful shapes that although stripped of a distinct image were full of dark murmurings that touched me from within. I slept little, wandering through my nights as though upon a directionless journey.

Most of the dreams revolved around Father Thomas's fable of a university of spirits, but dreams just as disturbing about the ever-changing Father Thomas surfaced as well, as though the bright infinity of my mind had been replaced with restless, dark waters.

When dreaming of the university I flitted through dim, vacant halls as though fleshless spirit, flesh harboring me again when I clamored down a raw stone stair into vast earthwork chambers stretching and turning endlessly, offering pleasure and deceits endlessly. Appearing in these dreams, Father Thomas was the specter I pursued, though when he turned upon my numerous pleadings I ran from him. All light had been evicted from my body; my mind had been returned to its prison of desires and expectations, which excluded and denigrated love. The spirit that had illumined the mind was beneath the stone of the mind's calculations. I again regretted all that I had renounced in order to seek the spiritual. I was even looking upon the riddle of Father Thomas and the prism of experiences at the seminary with suspicion. I wanted to be rational, sane, but was raging with spiritual fires, so I lashed out, disowning all that had been most endearing and heartening, including the priest.

I gradually acquired a passion for Zen because it seemed more firm and explicit in its practice, more a spirituality that nature ordained. And though I practiced just briefly, what I was most enamored with was the culture it had produced. I was again influenced to compose haiku, make ink brush paintings and carve wood blocks for printing. I had always conceived of my poems as a spiritual practice and so beginning to write haiku was a natural extension of that practice, though the haiku were more casual, much more natural in conception. I began sending them to publishers, looking upon them as Americanized Zen—which became a preoccupation for me, searching for a form of Zen that could be remade according to the spirit of the West.

I began sharing a house with James, an orthopedic technician in the emergency room. He had restored and mended a grand house in a ramshackle part of town. He was ever seeking to remake himself according to the tides of his spirit. He refused to be defined or to exist on the surface, but was exactly as he appeared, even his most casual traits issuing from his depths —he was governed entirely by what he imagined for himself.

James was a person who seldom read or conceptualized, but looked upon projects, such as remaking a house, as his spiritual path. James leapt into a project, depending on instinct, his heart over his mind, disregarding any advice or map. When he was working on a project it became almost a religion in which he worked to revise his nature more than actually to complete a task—a program most people found hard to appreciate.

Months passed as I shared room and board with James and we labored on projects, had wide-ranging talks that exhausted the night, or adjusted our pace and were out all night in the bars with the nurses from the hospital or members of my class.

College was far easier than I expected. In the two years before I earned a degree with honors in 1982, I for the most part managed to discard spiritual work. Sleep was a luxury not usually permitted, as I was in class in the day and worked the three-to-eleven shift at the hospital. Except for a rare trip to the seminary, I lived out a string of days in which there was no seeking or representation of spirit or light. All the vigor once devoted to spiritual occupation was bound to the splendid motion of work and play. The spiritual labors that had begun almost at birth had finally been disengaged and quieted. The burden had been unimaginable, the entire ordeal often invisible even to those I had lived with—but inescapable to me. There was no seriousness or exacting purpose within me. I wanted just to be happy, neither exceeding nor aspiring outside the human plane.

Gradually the indulgences wore on me and it became more and more apparent that I was an imposter, that even the lack of sleep and consumption of drink did not prevent me from longing for the spiritual, longing to see my priest again. Growing in me was the light that had once receded into an unimaginable depth—appearing just when sleep was breaking over me. I had intense dreams in which Father Thomas appeared, but they were masked with the drink I consumed many evenings. I never again had out-of-body experiences with the same frequency, and I attribute that change to this phase in which sleep was often so numbed that dreams seldom penetrated.

It was the autumn of 1982 before I met with Father Thomas again. It was most unexpected. I was in a tumbled-down garage discussing the wisdom of having the bearings replaced in my van. The mechanic suggested I have it junked and sold for parts.

I'll never forget. Father Thomas just walked out of the autumn afternoon and stood like an ancient prophet with dry leaves whirling about him. Never had I seen him in a formal priest's frock, and amid shades of black he appeared intense and full of purpose.

Though love can seem indulgent and weak, in Father Thomas it was neither. He was a being of love and conviction that outshone and overwhelmed his mere appearance. His purpose was to love.

Gravely he took my hand. "So on the eve of your graduation you have begun to avoid me."

Overwhelmed, I wept, and he drew me in, embracing me. "Listen to me. This lesson must sink in, it must be thoroughly understood. It is not difficult to have mystical experiences or pass through death. Human beings have a secret anatomy that produces the mystical and presupposes death. And it is even easier to sing hymns and mouth praises confessing love for God. But professing love is not the same as actually loving; the lover and the loved still remain apart.

"To love as God loves requires all that we are and all that we will ever be. We must abandon our personal story and accept God's dream as our own. This demands that the past and present be overwhelmed and born again in the fires of love. We must adopt this, though, not as a path but as a pathless simplicity. And to be so truly simple is not to be weak or indulgent; it is to possess a nature that is impossible to define. The nature of love is to move from mystery to mystery, loving without explanation and without a root cause. Because love is a mystery it cannot be defined—to explain love is to be apart from it. Within love is a motion that is so simple, so purposeless, that every complication that we have ever assumed and believed in finds its proper rest and harmony.

"Sinking into a trance we can assume the most quiet and pure aspect of a human mind. There is light and ecstasy and infinity of God quartered in a mere human being. Such a glorious light is a profound mystery, but so is even the most mundane human event—pregnant with the same mystery and suffused with the exact same light. So such a trance does not bring us nearer to God; God is near when we share in his will—then it is not important what we are seeing or experiencing. If we are outside God's will we are outside of God, even if we are burning with energy and light. And God's will is the most simple and profound of all—it is love.

"Rituals are just motion and noise, priests are registered on paper not in the heart; saints are marketed like spiritual toys. Churches make us afraid, afraid of hell and afraid we will not be among those chosen to be at God's side in paradise—so the parishioners seek paradise instead of just loving. We do not rejoice in God's love when we are just seeking his blessing; there is no praise God accepts except love.

"Seeing through our images and dreams, which include the dream of our senses, we are transformed into God. Putting aside our human will, our dream, our purposes, we become like a breath in the wind—in God's wind. Neither measuring nor judging, we exceed and sustain all, we both transcend and embrace in loving light."

He paused, lifting a single finger to his lips as though amused by his own passionate voice. I noticed then that he possessed all the features, all the changing attributes, that made me suspect that he was many men. For within his loving nature he was not pent up or bound as I was; he contained all of humanity and every possible experience because love does not exclude or judge. And there was no salvation for the human race except through such uncompromising love.

"Father," I confessed, "I have been weak and blind; I have odd, disturbing dreams; I am mired in regrets."

"I don't dream," he chuckled. "Or perhaps this conversation is my dream. For it is fleeting, vanishing even as it is happening. And subject to no more explanation than the most distorted dream."

"Father, I live with doubt; I am weak by nature."

"We are all weak by nature; that is what makes it necessary and possible for us to love. Do not struggle with your human frailties, just love and permit love to mend and remake you according to its purposes. When loves flows through our nature we are transmuted, but not perfected or just purified; we are in boundless motion toward union—God and world union. Love permanently marks and remakes us but it is not seeking our perfection; it is seeking to transform us into a form of love, a conditional representation of God's unconditional nature—all the rest is just adventure and appetite, motion and change. Do not contemplate your weakness; contemplate love. Give up all will; just love, just as you are."

Exactly then I noticed the weathered, grease-stained mechanic standing back, reluctant to approach the priest when he was speaking, but nodding as he raptly listened. Breaking off his conversation, Father Thomas tracked my gaze. Waving the mechanic forward he hugged me again, though he had become much weaker and during the embrace we hardly touched.

"Put aside all that you have experienced and mindfully examined, put aside all images of what you are. Do not look for God in symbols or among lights; just love God and all that he is presently creating. Then there is no doubt about it—you will be found."

And just as he spoke I realized this was what I was doing. I was overwhelmed with love just as I was usually overrun with ideas and urges, and this love was more personal and near to my heart than any image or idea I ever had. My body was overflowing and flowing into the priest, the garage, the orchard across the road. And I realized that life was a continual renewal; even death was just such a renewal. And I was willing to put aside all that had been dear to me, all that I had ever felt or imagined or assumed, all that I had looked upon as supporting and representing my innermost nature. In order to love I had to be renewed again, even until all that I had been was burned up, transmuted, remade. I knew what was required of me.

My longing for God had been touched by God's longing for me. And between these two longings universes whirled and constellations burned; all existence was at once set into motion and halted, sentient beings stumbling about in a maze of experience, finding and losing their companions. I had never fully realized what was requisite—to find God by loving what stood between us. We share God's vision when we are blind to our own. We cannot approach God through seeking or ritual, but through devoted and all-consuming love. And when we speak of love we are already speaking of God—no theology deepens or extends God's nature. This was the single approach possible—love until all that we have done and are doing is illumined and made transparent by God.

When I looked about it was all God's Light, it all belonged entirely to God, and all that assumed shape within it was thin and vanishing. Break apart shape and there is light; break apart light and there is love. That is the thought that summed up my realization.

As I was enduring the most significant revelation of my life, Father Thomas was walking toward a rusting pickup, which without a backward glance he drove away.

There would be much more required of me, much more to be endured before I made what Father Thomas suggested explicit in my being, for I was soon again enamored with the medium of the "spiritual" and the process of attainment. But the priest's resonance remained with me, guiding me, and through it all it was not a process of acquiring but of expanding my vision until it had the range to include what he asked of me that day. When we respond not with our wills, but with a spontaneous outpouring of love, then all that we have committed and desired is permanently at rest in God. This just God is our substratum, form, and the force of our being. This was what I was approaching, and each representation of spirit was just a sign that I was opening up, that my resistance was progressively being overcome.

Through the rest of my life I acquired a wider, more comprehensive experience of God, fording most spiritual paths and doctrines that have been created, but the process is of an extreme departure into mere radiant, unwilled Love. All Father Thomas's communications had been leading toward this—the force that underlies human mind and will must be made truly and unconditionally transparent to God. Regardless of the greatness of an experience or the inclusiveness and rightness of a particular realization, this is done solely from the point of view of the soul, the receiver of experience. The priest was demanding much more than this. The will, the pure intent at the foundation of all that is particular and human, must be submitted to God and overcome in the force of his light and the light of his love. Having many spiritual experiences is not to be gauged as a greatness. Rather, it should be looked upon as a refusal to submit to God's radiant love, necessitating that we need to be shaped, again turned on the wheel of experience. It is through a stubborn lack of love that we are called upon to exhaust all possibilities.

Chapter Seventeen

The Legend of Father Thomas

> *Behind the wound in Jesus' side*
> *the tomb of his heart rolled open*
> *and love's brightness poured out*
> *and was exchanged like bread.*

I began returning to share in the spiritual ambience of a garden set aside for meditation on the seminary grounds. Here the air was serenely composed, as though even the trees were in possession of a soul. Father Thomas did not appear, but my visits again returned to an almost weekly schedule. I was of a notion that perhaps Father Thomas was not even human. His last meeting with me had been so providential that I assumed he would contact me as he preferred, according to his inner designs.

Dee wanted to reunite and had been lavishly attentive, making wild, loving, and indecent proposals through much of the previous summer; in the spring, upon graduation from college, I moved in with her. The move was not merely a practical matter. I was again in love with her, though we debated the subject of marriage and children—I wanted children or there was no need for marriage. On all subjects except this we were of the same mind, quietly in love and sharing my first glimpse of a modest prosperity.

Just entering the profession of respiratory care, I began with a job at a rundown city hospital that housed the sick and disenfranchised. For the most part, the patients were neglected by the staff and treated as figures merely impersonating human beings. Murder was a frequent guest in the emergency room and I became intimately acquainted with the price of such rage apart from the dreams and movie images. As I circulated among dim wards of addicts and victims, I gradually, though unintentionally, retreated into a shell, for I was not prepared to meditate upon what I found—the rot, the pain, the humiliation was almost more than I was capable of enduring. Many of the habits I had once acquired were exploited in such an atmosphere, so I was indulging in drink again, though working against it. I was aware that to transcend the human condition it was necessary to become all or become voided, that a person must walk through experience or a person must retreat. I had been initiated into the extremes of human degradation and so, unconsciously at first, I began retreating into the mindless silence.

Eventually I was assigned to intensive care, a station of critical balancing acts and human despair. Though the patients were sedated into a perpetual twilight, pain was almost all that they were conscious of. Such harsh affairs contradicted my inner experience, so that to endure I had to be insulated. Just as much, I was affected by staff members who endured by remaining numbly detached from their experiences or sought to coat them with pleasure.

So I grasped the silence. And I rationalized, arguing that Father Thomas had encouraged me to uproot the mind and plant God in its place. Initially it was a relief to silence even the aspect of mind that witnessed and judged. Without judgment the mind did not strain against the silence and so it was a quiet, unremarkable transition. I assumed that my true nature and God's attributes were hiding among the objects of attention, whether among the province of the mind or the senses.

Dee and I found an apartment within miles of the old seminary. I reduced my hours at the hospital to part time, meditating and experimenting more with the silence. The apartment grounds were wooded and squirrels overran our patio. Eventually I opened the door to the patio and put nuts on the table for them. They climbed on the furniture and perched on the drapes. One squirrel in particular would actually sit in my lap and be petted. I purchased birds and a Basenji, a breed of African hunting dog that was ever testing my temperament. I insisted on a sleeping mat and a room kept bare for my use as this had always been what my temperament preferred, unadorned solitude. Each morning I put out seed, fed the ducks at the pond, or descended upon the seminary for meditation. Dee endured my phases and even warmed to my peculiarities.

Dee was both a fierce and bright aspect of a Tantric Goddess in the same body. She was exceptionally spiritual and a person of wide-ranging spirits and moods. Without her serving as my protective deity at this particular juncture in the spiritual journey, I would have floundered, for she had much more strength and endurance than I. She managed our practical affairs, permitting me a quiet, untroubled solitude when I was not at work. But more than this, she was consummately loving and reassuring—she had more faith in God's purposes than I.

The winter of 1983 I permanently set aside drink, but did briefly experiment with an hallucinogenic mushroom—readily setting that aside as well. On a morning visit to John Bryan Nature Reserve I ingested the mushroom as I walked the path. The path descended to a stream, where I stretched out to nap. When I awoke I was in, or hallucinated that I was in, a body skimming over the trees. Not until I swooped down upon a pond and heard my voice was I aware that I was trapped inside a wild goose. Such an experience was more than enough to terminate all such experiments with drugs, though throughout the rest of the day I merged into the earth and enjoyed a dark, womb-like repose.

Split, as we all are, between what is sacred and enduring and what enables us to manage and succeed in the world, I was just learning to accept and appreciate ordinary responsibility. I realized that extremes of pleasure or spirituality were equally unliberating. It had been my habit to reach for extremes, so that I was either engaged in being profoundly spiritual or seeking mundane recompense.

On a warm evening in the spring of 1983 I reached a decision and drove to the seminary. Lamps had been struck and the few tenanted rooms breathed out their ancient shadows. Watered-down shapes stood with the Virgin in the grotto and I waited on my usual bench for the priest until dusk was drawn into the earth. Just a week had passed since I visited the grounds, but now I was here seeking Father Thomas. I was prepared to lay claim to Father Thomas's friendship—to love and be loved.

I approached the entrance to the rectory and rapped on the door. When there was no immediate response I decided this wooden barrier required as much punishment as I could unleash. In the course of my banging a perplexed, dried-out-looking nun opened it timidly, turning her head slightly to look at me, then turning it further as though to edge me out of her vision. "Yes, sir, may I be of assistance?" she inquired in a voice that was formal but not timid, still harboring much of the music of youth.

"Is Father Thomas in? It is most important that I speak with him."

The nun was visibly startled. "Father Thomas?" she repeated numbly.

"Yes," I said impatiently, mumbling in an ill-advised attempt to describe him.

She interrupted my muddled speech. "You must mean Father Marcus. He is the only retired priest we've had stay with us."

"Father Marcus." I shaped the words carefully as my mind raced. "Would it be possible to speak with him?"

The nun's discomfiture grew as she squinted as though to peer through me. Finally she replied, "I must apologize. You see,

Father Marcus passed away two nights ago—in his sleep." She hastily added, "I must apologize again."

I stammered incoherently, both frustrated and coldly afraid.

"Young man," she addressed me, her manner suddenly quiet and inquisitive. "Where did you hear that name, Father Thomas?"

"That is the name I was given, by the priest," I blurted out.

"Odd," she muttered, shaking her head sympathetically. "But the old often do odd things, speaking from what they half remember, believing to have done what they dreamed or once heard."

I was stricken. Whether or not I had been deceived was of no consequence. In my despair all that mattered was that Father Thomas was presently intangible. The despair was not as much because of his death—that had been long expected—but rather was because I could not mentally invoke his image. He was truly gone, had vanished without a trace from my personal stage and the world's community.

The nun's voice was soothing, soothed as though she had reached into me. "The Father Thomas you speak of was rather a legend in this region. Perhaps he never really existed, but all kinds of peculiar stories have become attached to his name. Stories that describe him as both a saintlike figure and a kind of Indian shaman—he was supposed to have taken in Indian orphans during the Ohio wars. He was a renowned wanderer, performing strange miracles and expressing himself in strange, almost pagan tales."

She waited to see if I was listening and began again. "Among the stories that I've been told is that he befriended the Shakers, a sect of Christians that flourished on this property once. He danced their dances and sang their tunes. Then he would abruptly vanish into the woods and worship with the natives, engaging in their ritual dances.

"When affairs are dull here, which they most often are, we repeat the stories, usually in the evening, huddled around the lamp or a table. And perhaps we even amend them or add to them according to whim. For we have always viewed Father Thomas as belonging to us, and among us. I suppose that it could be argued that we have shaped him and he in turn has shaped us."

"Did Father Marcus take part in these stories?" I asked.

"Father Marcus? No, Father Marcus was usually not well and had problems with speech; he once had a stroke and his speech was halting. Most nights he remained in his room."

"Father Thomas never had a problem with his speech," I objected.

The nun stepped through the doorway and down from the doorstep and I found her slight, ancient, and quite beautiful.

Then we walked. We passed by the dooryard garden, which she mentioned was her private domain, past burning windows and out under the incandescent bowl of night.

Her voice was even more lyrical; she wrote upon my imagination as we strolled beneath the single dark motion of the night. Among stories she told was that Father Thomas carried with him a feather—to him an angel's single aspect visible to mortal sight, and the priest's sole confidant. But the nun argued against this version of the tale, asserting it was given to him when he was initiated as a shaman. Another story spoke of a birth mark that appeared in the shape of a rose upon his right breast, across from his heart. Refusing the trappings of a saint, he had muttered in protest that he was God's prostitute—that he had once manifested the signs of the crucifixion but had petitioned God for the miracle to be replaced with a sponge forever wet with fresh milk so that he could suckle the Indian orphans with it.

The nun laughed merrily as the legends spilled out, even apparently taking pleasure in the wild amazement with which I received her tales. "There was, I do believe, a Father Thomas. Probably a saint who attempted to intercede on behalf of the Indians and probably did not rebuke the Shakers as strongly as most of his patrons would have liked and so was branded a secret member of their cult."

"No," I objected, "I prefer the stories just as they are. What is the point of being critical? They will never be untangled."

"No," she agreed with a nod, as though an insoluble mystery pleased her more than a rational discourse.

Eventually we found my usual bench and she added weight to several of the legends, providing me with more stories. And each story seemed an exact reflection of the priest who had befriended and awakened me. But for all her familiarity with his stories, she was not capable of describing the man behind the legends, for it seemed there existed as many competing descriptions of him as there were tales of his life.

I returned the next week and the week after that, for at this juncture I needed these legends; they provided the sustenance and pure, untapped source of light I was so much in need of. Her love and patience burned much like Father Thomas's. It was as though her stories were not just about Father Thomas but of a shape he had assumed. It was plain that I needed those legends and so supported them. Even though it was not rational and there was but a slim prospect that the legends belonged to a man, or even many men, they were necessary to me then. And they remain an insoluble element of my character and view.

Each visit was spent beneath the transfixed statue of the Virgin Mary hearing a litany of legends. I exchanged my story of Father Thomas for her tales, my experiences perhaps destined to become legend as well. And when her legends finally were exhausted and my heart was full, we became friends.

Describing to me a brief visitation from Jesus she had had as a child, she explained her decision to become a nun. In the vision Jesus was a figure of honey white that tramped beside her through her father's field of corn. She longed for no deeper explanation or experience, nor did she apologize for the simple purity of those moments. Jesus was laying claim to her soul, announcing with his wordless presence that she was destined to walk beside him for her entire life. No miracles or visits occurred afterward, nor was it required or expected. She had been chosen for her life's work. Jesus needed say no more upon the subject.

In contrast, I had roamed the spectrum of vision and light, had been absorbed in trances, had even negotiated the passage into death, but not until I had met with Father Thomas had I found a life's work. My many experiences had just been a preamble.

Part Three

A Shoulder to the Wheel

Chapter Eighteen

The Tale Within the Tale

> *The Buddha flows*
> *along the river;*
> *and among the waves*
> *are many secrets*
> *once hidden*
> *in his breath.*

Dee and I purchased a home together and though we were not joined then in the accepted sense, we were coupled on the spiritual path we were treading. We accepted that we had been laboring to shape a romance from what was a deep, inborn spiritual link. With Father Thomas having vanished, I again returned to the deathless figure of Ramana Maharshi for support. Dee and I meditated together on the formless heart Ramana Maharshi had fashioned for the ages. The path he suggested was exceedingly plain and unadorned.

Ramana Maharshi: Can a man be possessed of two identities, two selves? To understand this matter it is first necessary for a man to analyze himself. Because it has long been his habit to think as others think, he has never faced his "I" in the true manner. He has not a correct picture of himself; he has too long identified with the body and the brain. Therefore I tell you to pursue this enquiry, "Who am I?"

You ask me to describe this true self to you. What can be said? It is that out of which the sense of the personal "I" arises and into which it will have to disappear.[7]

And upon the subject of the heart:

> Devotee: Sri Bhagavan has specified a particular place for the Heart within the physical body, that is in the chest, two digits to the right from the median.
>
> Ramana Maharshi: Yes, that is the Centre of spirituality according to the testimony of the Sages. The Spiritual Heart-Centre is quite different from the blood-propelling, muscular organ known by the same name. The spiritual Heart-Centre is not an organ of the body. All that you can say of the heart is that it is the very Core of your being, that with which you are really identical whether you are awake, asleep, or dreaming, whether you are engaged in work or immersed in samadhi.[8]

When I was meditating as he suggested, there was a downward push against a center in the heart that was analogous to the one he described. And gradually my meditation became a pressure down and against the heart that insured that the mind was clean of all motion and thought. When the energy from the heart was not permitted to rise, not only was the mind still, but so was also all the energies within the body as well. All neural and light channels of the kundalini were quieted except for those in the head, which became a form of pressure, especially in the middle of the head and in arcs that touched upon and moved down into the head from outside. The energy rested as a motionless, singular force, outside space.

Along with this, the blue *bindu*, or seed of consciousness as it is often translated in the literature of Tantra, appeared. In Guru Swami Muktananda's autobiography of his initiation and practice as an adept of kundalini yoga in southern India, this blue pearl, as he christened it, was considered to be the ultimate matrix of enlightenment. After my meeting with Father Thomas I could not put such stress on a mere experience as to presume that the blue bindu was enlightenment itself. But in my meditation that bindu would step outside me and I would meditate before it, as though at an altar.

Gradually the bindu became lighter, purified, until it appeared to be a white radiance that outshone all blueness. The preternatural brightness of this cannot be described and it was even more sensually alluring than in its precious blue form. But it seemed to me that the blue bindu arose from the head, while the seemingly purer, white light arose from the heart. This concept correlated with Ramana Maharshi's testimony of the soul at the apex of the heart on the right of the chest. It would be years before this matter was settled for me and the nature of soul was appreciated in its twin aspects.

Increasingly, my meditation duplicated that of Ramana Maharshi. Father Thomas had encouraged me along a similar but distinct path but had set no specific map to guide me. They both stressed love, and I was convinced that the priest would have approved of the Indian sage. Ramana Maharshi was just as impeccably compassionate, but stressed a silent meditation much more than Father Thomas, who spoke of opening up and becoming transparent to light.

During this time Tom, a lawyer with nearly grown children, moved into the neighborhood. He was quite spiritual and had studied with an Indian guru, though he was soon to become a spirit channeler and healer. We began migrating between homes as though we were part of the same household and I stumbled into a human glow that was foreign to me. I had been upon a spiritual quest almost two decades, and often destitute, nearly homeless. Now suddenly I had a home and loved and possessed in abundance. My rooms were overrun with his amazing son and daughter; whereas Dee was more connected with Tom, I was in love with his children. I again confronted all the regrets connected with the spiritual path, for I adored these children; in my heart they were the children I had always imagined.

I became ill and was hospitalized with queer, inexplicable pains in the naval region that I later deemed were from the naval chakra. The pains consisted of scorching heat which, according to the texts on kundalini, is an apt summation of the *manipura* chakra, the seat from which our fiery life force is generated. I theorized that my life force had been spent upon the rarified and blazing air of the spiritual, whereas Tom's children represented a humanized life force that warms and nurtures. Wanting to possess his children was an overwhelming urge which had to be exorcized, for it was a conceited love I desired to express through my own image rather than through God's inexpressible light. If Dee had wanted children I would no doubt have looked at this differently.

What finally put to rest this issue for me was an auspicious dream that was the vessel for a strange tale. It was in the mid-1980s, I had not seen Father Thomas in three years, and I had gradually begun to look upon him as a mirage, or hoax. But it seemed as though through the dream Father Thomas (or was it Father Marcus?) was returned to me. In the dream he was more fully present to me than he had ever been. Possibly it was just that he was present within my personal fiction and so I was able to mold him to my liking. Or perhaps he actually appeared in my dream, his appearance finally unrefracted by the senses. As ever, this dream was an opportunity for him to rhapsodize upon the nature of love. I formally composed the dream into a story, so that what I relate now is the tale that the dream became, for I have no memory of it aside from this.

The dream began with me at the hospital, though in this dream it was much like Father Thomas's university of earlier dreams. A few shaded figures traveled the halls, just at the edge of visibility. I was drawn to a room and there witnessed a death, and I was attracted to the next room where a birth was being enacted. Before the birth was completed, I departed, for I was familiar with, even bored by the process. Not until I was wandering on the next floor did I realize that the birth and death involved the exact same person.

I then wandered outdoors and breathed in the damp fullness of night. Galaxies seemed to be drifting over me. I noticed that the park across the road was enclosed in a fortress-like wall which had not existed before. The road had turned to cobble and once across I explored the space along the wall until I found a wooden gate that gave in to a mere touch. Within the stone enclave was a path. The path turned through the garden, turning upon the axis of a soaring cathedral. Approaching, I found it stationed upon the bank of a river. On its steps crowds waited. I hiked between river and cathedral upon sodden earth until I found a side entrance, which tumbled up a stair. I climbed through the skeleton of the church until I arrived on a platform suspended above every chamber and interior structure. The platform was bare except for a straw mat upon which Father Thomas squatted. He waved me toward him and then motioned for me to be seated across from him.

"I am delighted to see you," he began. "But be quiet and listen, for this is the tale within the tale and what the mystery is wound upon. For part of the mystery of existence is that it can never be fully explained and part of the mystery is that there is always another tale hidden behind the present one. Then again, perhaps I have said the same thing twice.

"You see, there was once a hobbling wraith of a hermit camping beneath a juniper in an inhospitable desert. The juniper grew the sum of the shade this land permitted and became like a dear friend to him. Just twice a month the hermit hiked to an herb-rich woods to gather remedies for his aches and the seeds that nourished him—and a share of the rich earth as a gift for the juniper that he loved and cared for.

"But on a particular day it happened that he had picked some magical seeds that, once swallowed, leaped back into his mouth and were so bitter stripped of their husk that they had to be spit out. And it happened that an alchemical change had taken place inside him so that wherever he spit a seed, an exact duplicate of himself appeared.

"Soon this cast of hermits crowded beneath the juniper, each more vocal than the next, each claiming to be the real hermit and the heir to the juniper. Even the original hermit forgot his true self and what had been his purpose, for he seemed to exist within all these bodies.

"A few seasons rushed by and all the hermits grew more infirm and it was apparent death was approaching. Each wanted to spend his remaining time praying, but all the hermits chose a different prayer and it soon became a competition, with God all but forgotten. Soon all the hermits stretched out beneath the juniper, too weak to even pray, death pouring its darkness into them.

"And then it happened. The original hermit remembered the day he began tending the juniper and his intention of nurturing it to become a specimen worth dying beneath. So his plans were rounded from end to beginning, except his memory was again dimming. Realizing he was about to again be lost among the mirror images created by the magical seeds, he grew desperate. Above all, he wished not to die lost and in confusion.

"Then it dawned upon him. He asked all of the hermits which of them claimed the juniper. They all began arguing, which permitted him to ask them a second question while they were distracted. He asked of them which among them loved the juniper fully and without expectation. Glaring at him, the company of false hermits faded away and the original was finally alone, his love for the juniper having proven his salvation. The hermit recovered and lived on until he was so ancient he looked to be a brother to the juniper."

For months I meditated upon the substance of the dream, which was the reason I wrote it out as a tale, to make it more accessible to read and reread. Much was garnered from my exercise—that to love is to be wholly present and exquisitely sensitive, so that the opposite of love is not hate, but distraction. When the hermit was not possessed of the images we all conjure, he was sensitive enough to again love the juniper, and so in loving, all illusion summarily vanished. The true self, or soul, of a person is that which loves and there is no insight apart from love, which determines the true soul from a false self.

What became evident too was that there is no misapplied love—to love a juniper is just as divine as worshiping God in this desert of human experience. Perhaps my path was more that of a hermit, but there are spiritual paths that lead through home, through marriage and offspring. All that is required is that we love faithfully and wholeheartedly; otherwise we are just imitating love—love that is bound by conditions or horizons is not love, and such love is preordained to be deceptive and fading. Perhaps the hermit had gradually become just attached to the juniper and so, through the ordeal of having to summon up and purge the false selves from his depth, he was freed so that he could again engage in a love that outshone mere attachment.

Over the years I reexamined this story repeatedly, and repeatedly it would reset my course when it seemed as though I had strayed. The message was there: we are all born to love and to see by love's illumination. By mere habit we are moved by false selves in a variety of disguises, but such selves have no real light or existence apart from what we project upon them, and so they must reach out and possess more and more to retain their hold upon us. If, however, the round of possessing is even briefly interrupted, the entire affair evaporates and the love that seemed ungraspable and the light we were shading begins to shine.

This story became a beacon which I set my sights upon, which I wrote and rewrote, pondered, meditated upon, and examined as though it were the words of my dear friend Father Thomas, which I believe it was. And the concept of a story as the most important product of this life became ingrained in me. For it was during this phase, as I was reviewing the writings of near-death experiences, that I happened upon the report of "life review." To me this did not represent a mere tallying up of deeds, but was a hidden tale that was being unraveled and relived. Witnesses to this life review at death described it as a replaying of their entire life, compressed into moments. Within this quick, transitional event was the kernel that was leading them toward a particular fate, for it was not the pictorial events within the story that were important but its motion, the need to "make up" or believe in a story to carry them across the threshold of death and even rebirth.

The entire momentum that leads us on is the story we carry with us: if we are reborn it must be either to continue the tale or so that we can embark upon a new tale it has inspired. So the process of learning in Father Thomas's university must be a process of assimilating our personal stories into the Divine's great epic, in which we love and empathize, heal and are healed.

My meditation became less a matter of fierce discipline than a relaxed flowering, less an ordeal and more a "taking of tea" by the soul's fire. Not that there were no trials, but they were expected and embraced as themes and aspects in my own tale. But what seems most crucial is that we look upon our tale as a mere story, one possibility among hundreds upon hundreds leading to God. Once a story is "unique," then love cannot resonate within it and it will hide its body of wisdom. I learned that we must just proceed along and illume the tale we have been born into, translating it slowly into God's story as Father Thomas advised.

It is also critical that we do not attempt to exchange our tale for another, such as by imitating a guru or sage we admire. For then our tale will be obscured and we will find no path to walk. As we love, all the dross of our story is burned up until all that remains is the bones of wisdom that were earthed within it. The ego, then, is just a reference point. The ego is "burned rope" as Ramana Maharshi once described it, still there but unable to bind us. We do not need to reach the completion of the tale, but just to scorch the tale with love and surrender.

Chapter Nineteen

The Death of Ego

> *Beneath the stone of love*
> *there is a light*
> *by which the ritual*
> *of Kali must be performed.*
> *The roots of devotion must*
> *be burned, not watered.*

By the winter of 1984 I had returned to Children's Hospital and was again working nights. In the month of December a lightning flash of an experience exposed for me the incandescence of no-self. I had assumed from reading the Buddhism of the elders that no-self was a state of relaxed ease in which the ego was just not engaged. I had not imagined that it was both subjectless and objectless, and that for me the most exalted of all Buddhist states would provoke a reaction of unalloyed terror.

I was at home and Dee was at work. Dusk was against the panes of glass and I was moving through the house switching on lights. I climbed the stairs to Dee's room, which was across the hall from my study, overlooking the patio. I walked into Dee's room and as I reached for her light any trace of a separate self vanished. In the hall I possessed a familiar sense of self and with a single step into the quiet sanctum of Dee's room there was no person and no mental references that were personal in nature; there was nothing to grasp, no hold upon my mind. Dee's room was familiar but I projected no identity upon it, nor did I sense her as a self, for not even the family photographs on her dresser were evocative. There was not even a remnant of ego in memory, for without a self to preside over it there was just an immeasurable present without distinct qualities or parts.

I had not been meditating, had not even been pondering a spiritual subject, but had been struck, as though by lightning. Reflected upon the closet mirrors was a human form, but I had no more care for that form than the lamp beside her bed. Bodily I had been divested of all self and those mirrors held an image with which I could not identify. There was no entity there; the body was just an appearance, a mirage in a room of mirages.

I groped for the rocker. While I was capable of movement, I was not capable of premeditating that move: there was no partitioning of experience and no self monitoring what was happening. As I rocked I attempted to recall a self, to refer to or assemble a mental image of a self, but it was apparent that such an entity had never existed except as a metaphor. I was merely present without relating to what I was experiencing. What my senses registered was unfamiliar because I was not imposing a self upon it. Mind was functioning, my senses were intact; it was just that there was no governor, just a subjectless realm of mental events and interpretations.

As I sat in her chair I noticed particles of light dancing throughout the room, sweeping from my leg to the carpet, to the chair. (Later I read that atoms leap between objects, perpetually joining and departing and it was apparent to me that this was what I had been seeing.) The entire room, including my form, was animated as a play of subtle energies. I was just one among many patterns of energy. Even the most insignificant particle in the room was in a state of unstable flux, changing continuously along the arc of moments.

Then the terror stuck me, a terror that was so primal that in retrospect I had to judge it as the essence of selfhood, for it marked the gradual return of self. There was no examination of this terror; it was just a mindless reflex as I gradually returned to being a precarious, pent-up, mindful self. This terror was the root of selfhood we live each moment. It rules over all aspects of human nature.

Fumbling with the receiver, I phoned Dee at work, explaining as calmly as I could manage that I had no self and was terrified. She spoke to me soothingly, evoking memories of a shared past, describing our best hopes. Gradually, through her voice, a self reemerged, then a functional ego, as the room returned to normal.

It was evident that I was not prepared for such a radical event. It was the same reflex that had gripped me during my death experiences, though I had not examined it sufficiently then to express it. It was not just fear, but our most urgent and primal response to our delusion of being separate from the Divine.

It was as though the light of this experience trickled down inside of me, for it remained a part of me. Events rapidly flickered across my senses, the earth breathing its forms; wherever I looked I saw the Buddhist concept of impermanence tangibly expressed. We were all being projected from and animated within a current of irreversible processes that is more like a magic show than a real event. I was not just living, I was being generated by an endless stream of processes.

Within months this perception matured into a more enduring insight. That spring I was returning home along the road leading to the seminary, though not with the intent of visiting. The windows to the car were down and I was meditating, locked in the mindless silence within. As I passed by the ruins of the Shaker barn, it suddenly occurred to me that I was holding onto awareness, that even during a meditation negating all forms of mind at the root of it there was an "I" holding awareness in its grasp. In the next breath I relaxed the grip and found that there was no self, no "I," but just an unbound field of consciousness that belonged neither in nor to the mind.

The self was not the mind or the emotions, but this core, this reflex to grasp even when all attributes of awareness were invisible. I suddenly realized that when Buddha was exhorting his followers to surrender their "grasping" or enter a state of nongrasping, he was not speaking metaphorically but pointing at the exact root of the self.

Perhaps a specter of Father Thomas was present. Doubtlessly he would have been pleased. For when I relaxed my grasp upon the interior silence, my nature assumed an expanse that included my form, the barn, the fields—a transparent brightness that belonged neither to me nor within me, but was just coincident with my human appearance. And this was, indeed, the same infinity I had experienced through Father Thomas.

It was apparent that the silence had never been the *lack* of being I had once presumed, but was the *support* of all being. For when I utterly relaxed I merged with a field of radiance that infused the silence.

When I returned home I carefully inspected my condition. Never was I more at home in the body. I could actually function and function happily in this state. The radiation of energy became a constant, and I was determined to begin a meditation that did not cling to or hamper awareness.

Finding that awareness had no shape and no interior or exterior was exhilarating. When I lay in bed at night, it seemed as though I was ever expanding. Thoughts arose, but there was no sense of being among them. Awareness and space and emptiness were the same. Though the practice would require much more work, it was eventually to be transmuted into love, for this meditation was an embrace, freely including and supporting all that it encountered, and when grasped or clung to it vanished. The wisdom that Father Thomas had wished upon me was born, though there was much that had to be endured before wisdom would persistently shape my experience. As Kabir, the "weaver of God's name," had so eloquently stated:

> A cage with ten doors,
> a bird of air.
> The wonder is that it's there;
> no wonder if it goes.[9]

A most odd experience occurred along the way. Seemingly the mind was turned inside out and apparitions, or visions, began materializing all about me. They included rudimentary and mythical images of the human unconscious, among which were ornate goddesses and sages, and numberless tiny Buddhas imprinting the air, the most potent vessels of this energy. Literally my mind was not within the brain, but was the atmosphere surrounding my body. I was reminded of the experience with the human aura and its dense population of images and thought forms, and it was apparent to me that we create the mental atmosphere within which we dwell.

I would often stretch out on the couch and just permit the images to arise, images that often as not Dee was sensitive to, so that she was prone to merging in the same condition, energies manifesting between us. It was not unusual to slip partially out of body, joining the images in "their universe." Gradually I learned that these images embodied energy that could transform, though Dee and I both regarded them with quiet reserve.

I noticed that the couch I sat upon retained these energies after the images had vanished, so that it was apparent to me that the home of a sage or his tomb could be a site of a potent transference. I had always looked upon the path of bhakti with a deep distrust, but it was apparent that in proper, loving worship of an image we can receive the energy that it holds. Because of this I began to consider pilgrimage as a vital aspect of the spiritual path and grew more receptive to the path of adoration of a spiritual figure and frequently pondered Father Thomas in this manner. As a result, there occurred a meeting with the priest that was more profound than any I had encountered in the flesh.

My composure was strained when in June of 1986 Father Thomas suddenly appeared before me. He did not attempt to communicate, but stationed himself at my side as had been his habit, purposefully regarding me. His mere presence, I was to learn, was a kind of spiritual disclosure. And so I attempted to accept his manifestation without being unsettled. I found that the more I concentrated upon him the more transparent his image became, until he vanished completely, or so I assumed. At this exact moment I was seized with an urge to sit in meditation posture. I folded into meditation and as soon as I closed my eyes saw that the priest had not vanished, but was within me, not just as an interior image, but as a presence that was assuming my entire form; I wept, realizing how spiritually impoverished I was despite my trove of experiences. Father Thomas's message had never affected me as deeply and profoundly as then.

When I looked down at my body it seemed to be that of Father Thomas, even to the patched trousers he had worn. I studied the ancient hands and bent root-like fingers resting on my lap, just as I had memorized them during our conversations in the grotto.

The room shifted, as though being aligned with an unheard and unseen dimension—a dimension in which light blew through the structure of my body. Then the mirage vanished. I was not to see Father Thomas again within the range of my vision.

I have often wondered if Father Thomas had been anticipating me upon those evenings long ago, for from the instant I sighted him it was apparent we were destined to meet, that I belonged to him. Perhaps Father Thomas had even been the dark figure in the transparent room of my death experience—perhaps I summoned him to me. But I realized that it was not Father Thomas himself that was important, or the boon of visions, but the unending gesture that Father Thomas represented, which was to love and respect and make of the spiritual journey a brightening, a fasting away in light of all that inhibits this wondrous process. Father Thomas, as my spiritual patron, remained reliably within as the innermost essence of my meditation.

I remembered that Ramakrishna once described the heart as "God's living room," and it was apparent to me then that it was the heart that we lived from, that was generating this person with whom we are familiar.

It was becoming more clear that there is no wisdom apart from love, for my wild experiences were not a spiritual triumph, but a burning path leading to God, which is love. Rather than merely to seek light and latitude within our human form, we need to unbind this energy and relax it. We cannot oppose the energy of death—that I had learned—we must surrender. And if our surrender is not voluntary, then we will be overwhelmed with the death process.

It was soon proven to me that this relaxation of self performed an alchemically rich transformation on the level of light. I found that during out of body experiences I was still holding on to a self, defining experience as I habitually did when in the physical body. But when I relaxed all hold on the subtle body it vanished into an enormous white glow. And when I returned to the physical body the entire room would be composed of the same white light, which was visible to me even as I consciously slept. Perhaps because of this realization, the entire dream process was transformed. Dreams were more fully lived and often as intense as waking consciousness. Dreams seemed to represent a reality that transcended personal existence. Dreaming became a form of meditation, a spiritual process which I came to depend upon.

I began to dream of a cemetery where Buddhist monks were waking up and teaching the dead. There were laborious crypts and passages within this cemetery where Tantric meditations were taught. The dead were rubbed with herbs and roused from an after-death slumber in their dream body. They were then instructed in a manner of transference of awareness where the monk bestowed upon the deceased the most holy of gifts—his own enlightenment. When the subject was "liberated" the monk retreated to a crypt deep in the earth to meditate and recreate his enlightenment so that it could be again surrendered. During these dreams, as a novice in their ranks, I practiced my meditation upon the dead, my body engulfed in visible light.

The process of dreaming grew gradually more pronounced, so that when I lay down and passed into the initial stages of sleep I often encountered dreams from years prior. Soon I had a recurrent dream that, initially, seemed of no particular consequence.

The dream was of a Christian monastery, located in the ruins of a city, which I visited with the tacit intent of purchasing. When I toured the site, it appeared to have just recently been deserted. Lamps with charred wicks presided over books spread open upon tables.

I repeatedly looked over the property until I judged it suitable. In later dreams I settled in, rearranging furniture and setting up a functioning monastery. Finally there were dreams in which I climbed, within the monastery, a tower previously assumed to be no more than a bell tower, to find a secret hive of rooms. I stumbled upon a cell where a monk possessed of a deep, spiritual nature had dwelled. The room still held his spiritual impression. I would sit at his reading desk, poised as though for his arrival. I was compelled to return again and again, sitting on his cot, touching his possessions. In subsequent dreams it became apparent that I was the monk and it was not until I stretched out on his cot and slept that the dreams stopped occurring.

A year afterward I happened upon a psychic in a spiritual book shop in Covington, Kentucky. A channeler was to perform readings for a group after closing and the clerk invited me to join. I was never attracted to channelers or psychics but it seemed a chance meeting that might bear significance and so I waited my turn as she reported on prior incarnations for the others in the group. I received a fascinating spiritual reading—

it seems as though I had been a priest or monk in every incarnation. She mentioned that in my most recent birth I had been a priest, and she described much that was coincident with my dreams. According to her I had been a Tibetan lama who had performed projection from my body at will and was not subject to ordinary death. She also claimed that I had been a Zen roshi and a guru in the Himalayas, but it seemed my most ancient and enduring link was to Tantric Buddhism. What was remarkable about this reading was that she was aware, or had stumbled upon, my predilection for death experiences.

Returning to my car that evening, I had to wonder—if I had always been such a spiritual man, what had happened to me? In what fashion had I squandered such splendid inner wealth that I now struggled so along the spiritual path? But I did not ponder the subject too long. Each titillating insight we receive is also a seduction, for it moves us from the point of wisdom into the field of ego's experience. Tibetan culture is steeped in ceremonies and internally structured legends, yet I had inherited a dislike for initiations and ritual observances; just as I distrusted any structure that is dependent on a spiritual adept.

Perhaps I am just too capricious by nature to appreciate such stringent practice. What I needed was the transcendent humor, the interplay and resonance of love, the soul engendered not by structuring, but by opening up and unstructuring.

I had stumbled upon a single force that supported all forces and energies, which was the love Father Thomas had instructed me in. What was required next was wisdom that would nourish me personally and permit me to review and preside over the process of opening. What I had not yet learned was that to achieve wisdom, energy and love must be married, that the deities of Tantra are not just ritually embracing and copulating; they are committed minds connected and hearts entwined, in the most enlightened sense of the word, married.

Still sharing a home, Dee and I were, at the heart of it, apart, having embarked upon paths that seldom met. Even our shared spiritual work was being uprooted. We made numberless attempts to mend what was happening, but when I wanted marriage Dee did not; and if Dee wanted marriage I changed my mind. Though we refused to examine it or admit to it, we were both attempting to uncouple. I had learned that spiritual pursuits and affairs of the heart are compatible, that romance and the shared heart is its own commendable spiritual path. But neither of us was ever the half that the other expected. It seemed as though I was merely a phantom, a projection of hers that I had attempted to become.

We finally agreed that we should begin seeing others. But it was not until Dee revealed that she was in love with someone else that I finally accepted the end of the relationship. Until then I could not imagine being apart from her. In the spring of 1986 we decided to permanently separate, rage spent, our hearts finally at rest in the inevitable. I could love her, but could not be intimate with her. Being intimate is a much more practical affair; this was an essential lesson for me to accept and act upon—love must be practical, must be rooted in the possible.

Chapter Twenty

Shattering the Emptiness

*Death amplified
over the mountains,
medicine of light
washed from my heart,
precious dreams just
ornaments in emptiness.*

Being apart from Dee was more traumatic than I expected, just as my spiritual work was not as firmly established as I had assumed. The incandescent dreams were no longer appearing. Energies were receding and the mind was growing quiet and fixed, as though I was again holding it inside a mold. This formless mold was the self, that which held "me" in and the energies out. I suffered a raw suffering that raged against spiritual work, against marriage, against all hope. I appealed to Father Thomas, but there was no response. And it was not until then that I realized that Father Thomas had been the soul of my spiritual journey, that in an inexplicable way he had been written on my mind and anatomy before I was born. I had been born to meet with him and I had kept him secret, denounced him in my heart, even betrayed his love in that I kept seeking an "enlightenment" that was mine, a state of rapture securely encased in a self.

In the summer of 1986 I experienced seizures of the heart. It seemed as though my heart were about to rise out of my chest, burning as it did. I could find no remedy, could not even establish a form of meditation. I raged at work and faltered along in my personal relationships.

Late that same summer, when I was at my lowest point ever, all motions of mind and self vanished and against my will I was again permeated with a subjectless emptiness, the self, or target of all experience, vanishing. I had no reference point, could not refer to or empathize with the personal trials that consumed the people with whom I interacted, and so was viewed as uncaring. This emptiness was even more bare, more penetrating than ever, without depth, seeming to be neither within the mind nor outside it, and holding my mind in a profound indifference. Wherever I turned I saw this same emptiness stifling all appearances. The world was robbed of all nuances, all that the self had invested it with, including pleasure and joy.

If I looked at an object, such as an apple on a table, what I noticed first was a pure immateriality to which the apple was fused—an emptiness that could not be conceptualized or examined. And this, not color or shape, not energy or mind, seemed to be the essential nature of the apple.

Even personal will was subjugated to emptiness. I felt a continuous pressure inside my head and splitting headaches—so restricted was my mind that I was not able even to look back on and examine my state. I was in a breathless void in which there was not a trace of religion or God or God's light. The reports of the senses, even that of touch, were toneless. Even the mind's voice had no personal tone or emotional context; in the same way, dreams appeared as bare, arid images. The world was muted and distant.

Never had I been so agonized. By late 1986 my resistance had worn down. Repeatedly I attempted to reconstitute my meditation by relaxing into radiance, awakening kundalini, intoning mantras; I even resorted to fervently praying to Father Thomas. But it seemed that all spiritual currents within me had been severed.

Such an emptiness is inconceivable to those who have never experienced it. It is to lead an utterly soulless existence, without warmth or hope. It is to be entombed in emptiness. All human beings, whether or not they claim a spiritual faith or uphold a belief in the human soul, refer all their experiences to the richness of an unconscious that is full of the defining elements and energies of the soul. So whether or not we consciously accept such a concept, we embrace it continuously. Inhabiting my mind was just silence and more silence. I was ever exhausted, wanting just to sleep, ever tempted just to stretch out and give in to the continuous undertow of emptiness. To be without a soul, to have no inner references, was to have a void where the mind contacted the world.

After many months, the first glimmer of hope dawned when a series of remarkable dreams occurred. These dreams possessed a warm, breathing ambience that became the sole spiritual treasure sustaining me. While I was awake, emptiness clung to my every motion. The dreams were of an ever-changing bookshop where I browsed, discovering books I had never heard of. In each dream I unshelved a particular volume which I would examine for the remainder of the dream, seeking to grasp the entire sacred formula the book represented and to absorb its essential energy. It was not unusual to wake up with an illustration in memory, or a portrait of the author, though I was seldom able to retain more than a fragment of text. Each book contained an image of a figure that was apparently a master, though not plainly originating from a particular spiritual tradition. The names of these masters were written in a vein similar to Sanskrit, though not decipherable by my accounts.

Despite these dreams and their significance to me, I was increasingly unbalanced by my predicament. Arising from the interior emptiness were random, wild moods. When these moods subsided I was exhausted and weak. I was prescribed tranquilizers. I acquired a sag in my back and a disjointed gait, as though my body was bending to conform to my inner state. At work I managed to seem fairly normal, but apart from work

I was quiet and remained for the most part in bed, huddled in upon myself.

What saved me was Julia. I had met her at work, in late 1986, when she was parting from a bitter marriage. I had been attracted to her since we had met, for she was just as charming to be near as to look at, her heart as rich as mine was barren. We rushed to rent an apartment and hurriedly arranged our lives around each other. Despite the emptiness that perpetually wove through all that I experienced, with Julia present it was manageable; when we were apart I was again ragged and desperate. I once again convinced myself that the spiritual path was the fever of an unbalanced mind. With Julia I recovered a measure of balance, as she provided a relaxed, undemanding love. Adopting her quiet and sane pleasures, I attempted to be rid of habits I had acquired in attempting to mute the emptiness. I loved her and her family dearly; I especially cherished the conversations with her mother, the vacations and holiday feasts—I had never been so embraced by a woman's family. We went on revitalizing vacations to the beach, where no demands or expectations were permitted. I had been pushing and seeking for two decades and never indulged in such luxury. It was a relief to presume that I was an ordinary person, seeking no more than what was most sane and pleasant.

When I was with Julia I experienced a respite, a romance that was simple, warm and human. I remained with her in that apartment for almost three years. And for a while the emptiness was partially set aside, held in with medications and the warmth we shared. But gradually it reasserted itself and when I decided that marriage was the cure I needed, the emptiness again swept in and I was within its yoke, even when I was with her. We had no fixed routine, so it was possible to be apart from her when the burden of emptiness was more than I could endure. I attempted to introduce her to—to explain—my plight, but she had no interest in matters that were not explicitly linked to the practical or pleasant. She was exceedingly loving and generous, but not a person who was attracted to that which signifies or explains. Soon I was taking more sedatives than I could count and was staggering mindlessly through my days. As a result, our plans quickly unraveled.

Julia moved out. Night upon night I counted my errors, sitting on the rug before an unlit fireplace. It was evident I had been both seeking my spiritual nature and attempting to disclaim it for decades. In suppressing the kundalini as I grew up, I had developed a rigid, almost indestructible ego. This ego straddled both worlds, but belonged to and was accepted in neither. All my spiritual work had been a raw exercise in ego. Even as I sat there, it was apparent that this ego was frozen inside the emptiness, as though firmly enshrined.

All of this became most apparent on a Friday night in December. There was sleet running along the porch, the wind roaming in the chimney. I stood in an apartment bare of furniture. And I was aware that a rare and precious opportunity had arisen, for I seemed to be shaking apart from within. I stretched out on the floor, breathing rapidly, prepared to accept whatever happened—even death. Not a shade of resistance remained within me; I could endure no more. The emptiness shattered, all mind breaking apart with it. I was spiritually naked and in an instant was flooded with a supreme, inestimable wonder, a wonder that was both the path and goal that lay beyond all conception and form, even beyond all formlessness.

I stood and whirled about the room, as capricious and senselessly human as ever. But an awakening had occurred. It would take me years to appreciate the subtlety of what had just happened. All that I was aware of then was that I was awake, at rest in a state that was neither mundane nor spiritual. I was not having a remarkable experience, for I was not having an experience. I just was. I was a fullness, a love and subtlety that could be neither mastered nor claimed.

The awakening never utterly vanished, reasserting itself again and again until I surrendered to its utter simplicity. For it was apparent to me then that realization was not a moment but a continuous process.

Chapter Twenty-One

Spiritual Rebirth

The tale is wordlessly
spinning in the heart;
a single lotus flower
transforms the darkness;
all of it flowing away
except for the river itself.

The next months were dedicated to finding a fresh approach to meditation. Silencing the mind did not undo the ego, but just held the ego apart from the world. Soon it occurred to me that the contents of mind were not what impeded the spiritual process; it was the entire context in which mind was viewed. So I attempted to re-view the mind without former prejudices and expectations. It was clear that there could be no actual, final, silencing of the mind without the dispersal of its energies in death. As long as these energies persisted, mind would have form and function.

The momentum of mind was that of a narrated fiction of an ego pretending to stand apart from the rest of the world. I had not taken Father Thomas's advice and had been seduced by my story of a spiritual wayfarer. But it was apparent that all such tales, spiritual or otherwise, were a poisonous stream. We are perpetually engaged in narrating "our" story and not in addressing what is most real. This book is just such an exercise. While the metaphor of the ego is entirely usable and necessary, and there would be no spiritual quest without it, we must not irrationally presume that the story is original, self-supported, and separate from the world. We risk becoming so caught up in our own tale that we believe it to be the only representation of reality.

It became evident to me in watching people who subscribe to particular religions, whether Christian, Muslim, Hindu, or Buddhist, that by nature all our tales and myths regarding religion are but rigid supports to our egos, and that our beliefs function as a precise map of reality. The truths we proclaim are elements of the ego's plot, keys to its survival. So when we defend a cherished religion, what we are defending is the ego's tale.

As I pondered the way in which Father Thomas had described making "images" and "story" transparent, I was struck by the ease of it—the ego barely existed and seeing through it was just a matter of fixing the mental gaze on what we usually presume can't be seen: the ego itself. If we just look at the ego without attempting to mend its appearance, it becomes transparent, with awareness shining through its words and images—the exact meditation Father Thomas had suggested. The ego is just a busy weaving of themes, images, and plots into what is presumed to be a single story, though no such singular narrative appears. The ego, or self, is always a work in progress.

But what Father Thomas had not explicitly explained was that the "images" and dreams are more verbal than pictorial, that the scenes are created more by words we use to describe them than by visual imagery. Most of the images he described were verbal constructs and most of the actual images were from a pre-rational depth touched with language. He never requested that I reduce mind to ashes; he just encouraged me to realize that my personal tale was transparent, a current in a river of luminance. When we awaken we are immediately aware that we have been dreaming. Once we have awakened there is no need to inspect or amend the dream; it is only when we are immersed in the dream's raveling that we need to seek God and project enlightenment. Once we are awake, the ego's rambling tale just has no point to it; we are neither inside it nor implicated by it. We can just relax and permit the tale to unravel at its own pace and not look upon it as "our" story, but the story of an ever-blowing spiritual wind which guides us all. According to Rumi, the visionary poet of north India:

> I've lived on the lip
> of insanity, wanting to know reasons,
> knocking on the door. It opens.
> I've been knocking from the inside![10]

Within this same time span I met Loree, and in October of 1990, outside on a sunny day on the grounds of a park, we were married. We then plotted our course toward New England, through the Berkshires, then along the coast, arriving at the island I love, Monhegan, where no compass is needed except for the heart. Here we confirmed that our marriage was a preamble to a joint spiritual quest.

I was fortunate in my choice. To have such a wife is to possess love's mirror and engage in a spiritual marriage that is part spiritual rapture, fiercely held and sung. Such a love is an artwork, requiring the embrace of an ever-aging body and the sight of ageless eyes. I talked with her of spiritual matters I had not spoken of in years, and she provided me with support and courage to push on, to seek the majesty at the heart of all spiritual matters. And in return I was bearing testimony that such a spiritual path existed, that it just required patience.

I supposed that the passage through emptiness had been drawn out because I had resisted it, that I refused to acknowledge what was most implicit: the mind could not be bound except by the mind itself. Silencing the mind had been the mind's work; mind had never disappeared; it had just taken on a single task. What had been most required was *community*; I needed the impetus of again sharing my spiritual needs, discussing and exchanging them in order to detect a passage through what appeared an impenetrably barren silence.

Also a respiratory therapist, Loree had been working at Children's Hospital for a number of years, but I had rashly judged her, fifteen years younger than I, as too young to engage in sober talk. And she possessed a rare beauty which just as irrationally I presumed excluded depth. After I met her it became apparent that my spiritual "past" would always be with me and that I could not hide or just disconnect my spiritual inclinations from my relationships. Our culture represses transcendence and so I had hidden my pursuits, as though ashamed of them, pretending to be part of the usual social current.

At work one night my duties were reassigned to newborn intensive care, Loree's sole province these past years. In the course of working at her side I found in Loree a poignant, extravagantly bright and spiritual person who had been groping, searching for a path. As I put it then, "her heart was in order." She cherished what was important to me and yet had a candor and practicality about the spiritual that refused to be deceived.

When we married, Loree moved into my cramped apartment. And she cleaned me up. I again—and finally—quit smoking, and adopted a vegetarian diet. I was again sane and breathed in relief; I had endured and returned intact, had been shattered and remade. Loree and I were both lovers and a pair of monks sharing a spiritual cave. I had once separated spirituality from ordinary affairs, from community and family, assuming that my experiences bestowed upon me a destiny that could not be shared. But now I saw that progress made upon a foundation of love and harmony was the only metaphysical truth, requiring us to be shamelessly and tenderly human. Especially in regard to the sexes, for our husbands or wives are our hearts' emanation, and the path of relationship unwinds directly into the sacred. But if one's lover is not spiritually embraced, then relationship becomes a competition and a cruel mirror.

Just after Loree settled in I had an enriching meditation that both shed and revealed light—rare that both are provided with a single experience. On the subject of dreams it expressed a secret within a secret: that subtle energies and events are infinitely malleable, but are not therefore any less "real." They express discrete events just as corporal events do; it is just that this expression is speeded up, mutating more quickly than it does in more apparently physical realms. This was the account that I wrote just after the vision occurred:

> I was stretched out, meditating upon my back, when a lightning rush of energy ascended the spine; I began shivering all over and my body was literally dancing on the mat. Then I found that I was in a car on a highway that was ascending along the sharp course of a mountain road. But the car vanished, and I began walking along the road, which was apparent then as just a path between boulders along a mountain pass.
>
> Once I arrived at the summit of the mountain my body assumed a huge stature and I was able to stride over most of the terrain that lay ahead. I soon found a path more suited to my stature and began running, half levitating, as I approached a lush estate that was a formal institute with an elaborate arch at the entrance.
>
> As I approached, a guard rushed toward me with a huge beast at his side, its nature and physical stature ever changing. It was apparent to me that I could not see it as it really was.
>
> I was embarrassed and slightly afraid. "I'm sorry, is this private property?" I inquired.
>
> He answered, "It belongs to all, but few find their way here. Come along," he added as he trotted back toward the estate.
>
> He had to wade across a stream to return, but when I stepped in behind him it was deeper, more hazardous than I expected, and I floundered in darkness until I utterly

relaxed and was swept across. I recalled then that when crossing over into the higher, spiritual realms there is a band of darkness that must be crossed, and I was seeing it just then as a stream. I was projecting upon this a form that I was familiar with.

The grounds were wondrous and I was immediately ushered into a building. Inside the air was lit with energies. There was a figure who was apparently in charge, but the energies made it impossible for me to fix my gaze upon him; he shimmered in the haze of his own energies. Father Thomas's name leapt to mind and I reached toward the figure. But I was swept back by the crowd within.

Just then a shattering energy swept upward through my body. I glanced toward the figure as I toppled to the floor. The energy held us all; whether we were animate or inanimate parts of the room, we were all conscious and singing with the fullness of this energy—the like of which I had never encountered in a kundalini meditation. This energy was not just force, it was the breath of love itself.

Just then a woman approached and began kissing me urgently and deeply and I glanced about to see if this was permitted. I could not resist the energies being exchanged and kissed her passionately in return. The love rushed back and forth, as though we were breathing it into one another. There was music too, but it seemed to be part of the atmosphere and whenever it changed, the energy in the room changed, and we each responded. At this point the figure of the teacher leaped upon me from behind and pressed down at the base of my spine on both sides. Immediately I felt as though my spiritual heart had expanded and I was inside it. There was no kundalini, no form or condition within this energy; it just loved, embraced, expressed.

I then was ushered out with the rest of the crowd. It was then that I noticed that the woman I had been kissing was my wife. A friend of mine who had recently died of AIDS appeared on the other side of me. And the terrain about me began to transmute, becoming unreal. I was creating it and recreating it with my mind, but it was apparent that my wife and friend were quite real. I asked my friend if he would return to the institute but he replied that he had much work to do, many habits that constrained him. Then he hugged me and vanished.

I heard a gentle sound, like a thread snapping in my spine and I was again in my body, stretched out upon the mat, arms and legs numb. I rushed in to look in on Loree—she was in bed asleep.

The vision was perfectly retained, as though each detail were a mark that had been left upon me. The energy had risen along the spine, but in its most important aspect was apparently unconditional. We project our ego onto experience, bestowing upon it a framework that is all but invisible when we are within our physical body. It was this projection to which I needed to put an end. This was where my meditation was to begin afresh.

When we are in an awakened state, the energies are noticed more as a "fullness" that is at the root of even the most ordinary affair, but cannot be grasped or claimed because the ego is not in power. In the nonawakened state, the ego exerts power over these energies, manipulating them, holding them in. This power is the ego's constant, obsessive pursuit, either conscious or unconscious. Greed for pleasure or spiritual experience is the same manipulation of energy.

To not be "in power" is to initiate a healing process, for the energies are not cramped or distorted by ego; they are liberated to express their true nature. And as part of my healing I began to reexamine the ordeal that my spiritual past represented. I began taking notes in an effort to make sense of the imbalanced aspects of the spiritual journey. Loree helped me by commenting upon them practically, without being impressed or drawn in by the various experiences. When we sat in meditation and I demonstrated the transmission of shakti to her, she was able to look upon it and speak about it objectively. She would frequently inquire, "But what is the point of it? In what way does it enlighten?"

In finally and irrevocably emerging from the void with which I had struggled for two decades, I found my outlook and mood transformed. I was writing again and the material was lush and rich with praise and images; it was as though I had just emerged from the colorless void into a realm of pure burning color. I wrote poems in inebriated flourishes and then tossed them out, for their brightness quickly wore out. They bore only a slight resemblance to the light that haloed and permeated experience.

Again my senses were permeated with an unconditional, unpolarized light, but different from before in that it was neither subject to me nor referring to me. It was just the unalloyed present: a transparency that smoothly encompassed whatever appeared. When our personal tales and images are translucent and the heart of experience is rendered visible, when we no longer project our person upon the world, the world is possessed of undying light. Meditation should be just a process of airing out the ego, permitting the mind to shine rather than invert upon itself. As my ego was made transparent I found that I was compelled to love. I became a person with whom I had not even been acquainted. My habits were quieted, purified, and my thoughts became calmer and sparse. Love and light were magnified, as though through a lens.

But there were effects that required a cautious approach. For if the mind was spare of thought, what thoughts did arise were subject to more intensity, so that if I was not mindful a single thought, whether positive or negative, could utterly consume me. Deeply buried in the residue of mind were rages and desires that were being dredged up. I was prone to anger and sudden outpourings of sentiment that had no apparent source. All that had coagulated within the mind during those years I had silenced it sought to be expressed. Mind is made powerful when we are awakened; if we trust the remnants of ego that remain we are prone not only to mistakes but also to delusion.

I was groping forward in this awakening, playing hide and seek with it. I realized that we must mature into awakening naturally, slowly. I found that I was able to release all hold upon the field of the mind itself. Then the inner infinity that I had once experienced with Father Thomas reappeared.

These were the most subtle states I had ever encountered, but still they could be held onto and examined as mere experience. Even the condition of radiation, or light, was graspable and could be defined as "an experience" that was related to a host of similar experiences. When I had awakened there had just been an unconditional state which could not be held, examined, or set apart as mere experience. The ultimate realization, I was sure, must be a revolution in consciousness and not just an experience consciousness is having.

Because my awakening had begun to penetrate the stages of sleep, I learned much about its process. Awareness is not as confined in sleep as we assume it to be. There were nights when I remained aware throughout the stages of sleep, in resonance with my surroundings even in deep sleep. Most remarkable, just at the brink of sleep there was a recurrent appearance of a pale, almost lunar glow lighting my head from above. At times the light appeared to be at the end of a tunnel, much like those described in many near-death experiences. This in particular provided me with more evidence of the twin nature of sleep and death: that in sleep the dream body or "subtle" body detaches itself just as in death. Whereas the earlier kundalini-generated experiences were more peculiar and disjointed with a quality of raw upheaval, these sleep episodes had a distinct spiritual texture, far richer in tone, much more intriguing, and seemed to be seeking to join me to wisdom and not just engender more experience.

I readopted the meditation on radiance, or love. The crucial mistake which had abruptly returned me to the emptiness was made apparent. The meditation began as a sheer pleasurable radiance without a perimeter or center, but as the ego gradually took over the meditation I began to purposefully radiate.

Soon the enterprise was steeped in the ego's needs and expectations. As I radiated willfully, the point from which I radiated became an egoistic constriction. The more I then attempted to radiate, the more my interior was restricted and held up, stifled. In my case, such effort was produced that all energy was utterly stilled.

Now, as I returned to this practice, it was apparent that I just needed to relax; if I was intent on expanding into light, then I would again unwittingly constrict the energies. I discovered that the attempt to expand energies was as much the ego's trap as suppressing or silencing energies. The innermost energies are trapped, or held in place, as much by expansion as by suppression; there is a stricture at the root of it that is holding the self apart from the rest of existence. Merging with radiance is dependent upon relaxation that seeks to love and embrace what is present, not to outshine or exceed or change what is.

A final dream of Father Thomas in March of 1992 established for me a spiritual covenant. I was walking from the Children's Hospital toward a walled-in forest. The dream was stirringly reminiscent and I was serenely attracted to the forest, scaling the wall and hiking the tame woods inside at a rapid pace. The wood was graced with gardens and formal hedges, with polite, meandering streams, as though it were an estate worried over by a host of gardeners. Soon I was approaching the familiar tower of my earlier dream. It was broached by a sonorous river. I skirted the tower, clamoring over an arched bridge and stumbling through a timber door. I entered and climbed a structure of wooden stairs and platforms, planks, and scaffolding. I noticed that I was grasping a book, which then vanished. I ascended until I arrived at the crowning platform in the heights of the vast church tower. On the platform a man in clerical robes was seated on the floor. When I arrived he bowed and as though engaged in a ritual poured a cup of wine, placed it on a linen scarf spread upon the floor, and gestured that I should drink. I drank and he bowed again. Then I awoke.

I recorded the dream, though I have rewritten it since in an attempt to recreate the beauty of the scenes that I witnessed. But what was most important was that even though I had not tacitly recognized the cleric in the dream as Father Thomas, it was plain that a peace had been struck with him. Clearly we had engaged in a Christian ceremony; what was not so clear was whether or not the ceremony was in my honor. But, for whatever reason, I found the dream richly satisfying.

Episodes of nonexperience began. I would be laboring over a task, or even reading, and I would glance about to find that all self had vanished. And when there was no self it was apparent there was no need of enlightenment, spirit, work, or development—the self was the axis of all such preoccupations. The entire affair of spiritual attainment was entirely dependent upon a self. I was not even registering an emptiness, as this would demand that attention arc back upon the mind, which was not present and could not willfully be produced. This experience was not supported or acquired through concentration, there was no approach or path toward it; nor could it be deepened or broadened, for it was not a matter of obtaining or grasping, but of releasing all grasp. There was no self because there was no reflex; my reality was at rest.

As this state appeared, vanished and reappeared more frequently, my approach was transformed—I was not seeking a path, or even enlightenment. My goal was to heal, to sustain, to become an unsentimental lover. If love was not implicit then I was not concerned with even the most magnificent prize the universe had to offer. I was not concerned with my bitter karma or my plight, or even God; I just wanted to love and remain posited in the wilderness of suffering. There was no work, no project, no ascent, except in extolling love and love's grace.

Chapter Twenty-Two

A Sacred Vocation

> *My karma this night:*
> *a mountain leaps over the universe,*
> *a sutra drowns the ocean,*
> *a rickety bridge leads to God.*
> *Awakened by the pleading wind*
> *the Buddha is upon the plain;*
> *his immaculate shoulder*
> *once again upon the wheel*
> *of birth and death.*

Migrating among roles in hospitals since the age of eighteen, I have repeatedly met with both rage and a magical unfolding at the approach of death. During the year that spanned parts of 1993 and 1994 I had a last experience that placed me firmly in what Tibetans refer to as the *bardo*, literally an "in-between state" that is neither life nor death. I also witnessed the deaths of three friends, which broadened and deepened my appreciation of the process, for they spanned the spectrum of responses to an agonizing ordeal we must all endure.

We are all stripped naked by death, releasing our grasp on

what is unstable and temporal. As with any genuine, heart-inscribed spiritual passage, death is a storm and a test that requires profound surrender, the sole test we are born to. According to all I have met with, death is just ego-death. All that is annihilated is the surface, or ego-field; the wordless reservoirs of mind not even disturbed. Death is the culmination of the life's spiritual process. To surmount death we must either be unfettered by the ego or the ego must be bound to its love of the Divine—this is perennial wisdom. We can either be so penetratingly wise that no hallucination seduces us or be so enamored with the prospect of God's light that we make an unequivocal leap, even an infinite leap, at death. From birth far into death, all we meet with are hallucinations and passing shows upon the light of consciousness. If we are attracted and compelled by that light then we are safe in the arms of our own being at death, our desire transmuted into incomparable joy. Or so I have concluded.

Presiding over his mother's death in a manner reminiscent of *The Tibetan Book of the Dead*, Ramana Maharshi described it in these terms:

> Innate tendencies and the subtle memory of past experiences leading to future possibilities became very active. Scene after scene rolled before her in the subtle consciousness, the outer senses having already gone. The soul was passing through a series of experiences, thus avoiding the need for rebirth and making possible Union with Spirit. The soul was at last disrobed of subtle sheaths before it reached the final Destination, the Supreme Peace of Liberation from which there is no return or ignorance.[11]

In 1994 I happened across a new translation of *The Tibetan Book of the Dead*, by Robert Thurman, that was like a stream of grace. His exposition on the tantra of death supported and made legible all that I had endured. Death was unmasked as all my studies and experiences converged.

The Tibetan Book of the Dead, or, in more accurate translation, Liberation Through Understanding the In-Between, elucidates the process of death and the pre-rational and irrational impulses that link us to rebirth. Death's shattering unleashes a fury of inconceivably wild energy winds which have structured our ego. We pass through the real, lucent, or diamond-like light of realization and into the raw energies and peripheral lights of a "void." If we are aloof from the raw impulse of mind, or are attracted to the transparent light (God), then we are liberated and death is perfectly and absolutely resolved. It has been my experience that what repels us about the "real" light is a supreme intensity that repels the grasping and controlling ego. The ego refuses to be subjugated to God's light, which is a light that is not just radiance, but the most primal of all forces and conditions and will reach out and attempt to seize us and reassume us at death. We will be compelled by ego to resist, and it is quite simply in the process of resisting that we are reborn.

It is all the constellations of death, the images that the "energy winds" of Tibetan tantra conjure and reinforce, that we will be attracted to and that will inspire us to return to our ego, though an ego transformed with rebirth. The ego cannot blithely continue but is called upon to be shattered and reassembled in the irrevocable death process. This is what I concluded from my numerous death experiences and decades of studying meditation.

According to both the texts on Tantric Buddhism and the scriptures of the age-old *Upanishads*, there was considerable support for the heart as the seat of the soul. And, according to the Tantricism of both Hinduism and Buddhism, there are two "drops" or bindus. These are matrices of awareness that comprise the soul—the primary and less personal indestructible drop residing in the cave of the heart and the personal soul hidden in the core of the brain.

What was most fascinating to me about the process described in the Tibetan sources was that they see the nerve pathways and energy channels as the true human vessel. And on these pathways there are subtle "drops" and the most subtle and indestructible drop is located in the heart and is the pure, transparent light, or soul of our being. It is the light to which we must be attracted if we are to succeed in death and not merely be mindlessly passed into rebirth.

There were even descriptions of the manner in which the drop in the heart is entangled or held in, so that "a sixfold heart knot" must be unraveled at death. If the knot is gradually relaxed and untangled during a person's life, however, then death will be a natural unfolding—there will not be a sudden wrenching apart of our subtle structure and the energy winds will not rage. I was elated when I read this—for I had discovered that the paths of love and realization coincide and relaxing the knot of the heart was a meditation with a respected precedent.

According to what my meditations had accidently garnered, the white bindu resided in the heart and could appear as a white star with five points, which is confirmed in Indian texts as indestructible Brahman, both smaller than the smallest seed and larger than the universe. The exact nature of this drop, in other words, is unimaginable. The blue bindu, as it is described in Indian Tantra, is the transcendent soul. At death, or in profound meditation, these lights merge, the star appearing within the vehicle of the blue bindu. The purer the meditator, the paler or more lustrous the blue bindu appears; for a soul that is impure it may even appear black. But in the course of meditation the blue bindu may either become so pale, or the star may appear so bright, that the blue bindu or soul is eclipsed by the pure white star. According to the texts on Tantric Buddhism of Tibet, the objective experience of consciousness is either transparent radiance or white light, while the subjective experience is formless consciousness—when they merge there is liberation.

Despite my newly harvested convictions concerning the death process, I must affirm that when working with the dying it is essential to remain within the framework of their personal beliefs—to do otherwise would only compound their traumas and make more elusive the subtleties of death. We cannot prepare a soul to pursue and retrieve a heart drop in a wild, untamable void. But the more we interject love, in all its aspects, into the process, the more benign the transition into and through death.

This became for me a consuming endeavor—to learn to protect the dying against the sheer range and intensity of the death experience. For the so-called seeds of karma cannot just be renounced; they must be met with and wisely dispersed. In other words, we must be anxious to embrace God and God's light. If we love fervently enough then death is a rapture, in the sense of its root word, which translates as "to be carried away."

Ego's story arises on the subtle level as just a flow of energy. This path will produce a rebirth; and though the ego will be remade according to the gross form we have assumed and its conditions, it will remain the same flow of energy. If, however, we prefer to flow with love then there is not a random rebirth. It is the pursuit of a personal fable that plunges us into the currents leading away from God.

I began to ponder the fate of a "realized" soul, or what is referred to in the earliest forms of Buddhism as a "non-returner." In the later tantra this is described as a magic cloud of harmonized consciousness, an enlightened sheath subject to the sheer bliss of liberation. Although I would not presume to have attained this state, my death experience when I was transported toward God in a state of bliss seems to correlate with this. All of it was plausible to me except for the laborious rituals; I was moved by the tantra of Tibetan Buddhism but not moved enough to embrace it fully in its traditional framework. And looking upon the recently deceased as spiritual voyagers and not haphazard victims revitalized my work with patients.

Caring for the dying is a noble, heart-shaped art in which we share in "being carried away," never forgetting that the purpose of death is to soar from life's restraints. But in order to be of support we must accept all the primitive odors, textures, and repelling sights as though they are ours, as though death is just as equally upon us—which it is. We must explore that process with deep trust and endurance.

It was in my caring for a dying patient that many of the spiritual, inner events related to the death process began to unfold. There are many echoes as we die; the energy that is usually bound within us is unleashed, and despite frailties and conscious liabilities the death process unravels the energy matrix and we have a heightened sense of spiritual immanence, light and love. To begin with, I had assumed that to love during the death process was just to care for the patient inexhaustibly and carefully. But gradually I became aware of a flow of energy that was initiated by the death process, the energies from both above and below gathering in the region of the heart. The heart is the binding core of the human spirit and the repository of love. And love should initiate an untangling of all the confusing and selfish energies that have been brought to the spiritual heart for that purpose. It was evident then the reason that Father Thomas's "hidden message" unfolded within my heart. My entire life had been a paradigm in which love and death were met with and mutually resolved. And so as I worked externally with the dying I also worked internally, transmuting the welling fires of light and mind with the sleepless, all-enduring love that is ever rooted in the heart.

At death all consciousness, mind, and vitality are turned to the heart. Through my consciously linking them to my heart, energies were mutually melting and being purified so that at death the energies would rise and depart forcefully toward higher realms. For once you have genuinely loved or been loved, you are spiritually linked. And at death, when the physical body falls away and then is made transparent, love outshines all other energies and considerations, so that we are inevitably attracted to the light. My meditation is then finally translated from the heart to the apex of the skull, the opening to the highest domains.

To a dying person we should appear as a lover—not as an expert or charitable saint, but as a vessel through which the echo of their human nature is returned. Death is a sacred ritual which we must engage as such, our skills and resources only supplementing compassion. If love smolders in us as we perform our tasks, then perhaps it can be translated in such a manner that it can be invoked by that person in the bardos of death itself. Touch is most evocative and the more we practice it, making the dying person into a map of our affections, the more they are reminded of their precious nature—and it has been my experience that whatever image we possess of ourselves is amplified in death. Despite the wisdom I have gained working with the dying informally over past decades, I have not always been able to apply it with the equanimity and heart that I have described—there have always been lapses.

Pain is the most ancient benefactor of spiritual wisdom. Innumerable pains march us along the spiritual path and lay siege to us as death approaches. We are either transformed by pain or we are conquered; it cannot just be passively endured as many naively assume. No meditation has been legitimized until it has met with raw, insoluble pains. Pain is both our apprenticeship on the spiritual path and the test at its conclusion.

Years ago I was hospitalized for inexplicable pains, as though I had ingested poison or burning coals. I thrashed in the bed in a rage of sheer, unblemished pain. In this state all I had held as dear and personal was made insignificant; the pain was a furnace that burned away all sentiment and illusion. Even then I was versed in meditation, after the fashion of both mindfulness and concentration, but neither prevailed against the pain.

But there was a wonderful lesson to this experience. I had been admitted to an indigent ward for lack of space, and as I thrashed about a patient left his own bed and spent the night clutching my hand and mumbling reassuringly. His ministrations soothed and by next morning the pain was manageable; it was as though a blessing had been transmitted by him. When I regained health I sought him out, expecting to find a saint. But what I found was a mildly retarded man with a cruelly deformed spine, unwashed and ragged. But his embrace was so warm and genuine that I wept. I realized then that the nurses had rained no warmth or love upon me; I had been punctured, radiated, medicated, and shunted about as though my feebleness had made me a ghost. But a stranger's care had penetrated the haze of pain and had communicated that any human gesture alloyed to love is right and perfect. His is the image I retain when I provide care for the dying.

Death is a process of reaching out and assimilating, trusting and patiently enduring, or it becomes an agonizing madness. When death is sinking into the human mind there is no wisdom except love. Pursued in all our tasks, quietly relaxing with us, love must be an unflinching endorsement of all that is miserable or frail about being mere flesh.

Adding poignancy to these lessons in a brief span, three friends died, all afflicted with cystic fibrosis, a disease that cripples the liver and attacks the lungs with fluid. Each, though a young adult, was in a children's hospital because they had been diagnosed and treated there as children, their disease familiar primarily to pediatricians. We received such patients from all over the state because of a wonderful doctor, perhaps a saint, or maybe even, as I have often imagined, a Divine Mother, laboring incessantly to make their ward into an island of compassionate and skillful medicine.

* * *

Janet was almost weightless, blonde; she liked to talk, her mouth churning expressively even when she slept. She either raged against or passionately loved those who provided her care; there was no meek acceptance. From the time she was a mere child, I had cared for her, loved her, and upon occasion endured her. Many a night I had carried her to bed in my arms. In the months leading to her death she accepted Christ as her saviour and listened to tapes of scripture as she lay weak in bed. At her request I bought her a book on near-death experiences, but we never explicitly discussed it. Many nights I lay beside her in bed and watched television—we would agree on a program and she would page me when it was time for the show to begin.

Normally I worked in the pediatric intensive care unit (where Janet was then a patient), but one night I had been transferred to the nursery. At about four in the morning I was notified that she was doing poorly. When I arrived in her room she was hunched over a stack of pillows, gasping. I would have remained at her side but the resident physician on duty had written an order to put her on mechanical life support. Janet and I had discussed this and she had been adamantly against it—yet had not drawn up a living will. Managing to delay the procedure, I phoned her parents, then her private physician, relaying messages for nearly an hour until the matter was finally settled.

When I returned to her bed, Janet was unresponsive, her respirations exhausted and her heart rhythms weakening. Except in a hunched, sitting position, breathing had been impossible the past weeks, so I climbed in bed, hugging her and supporting her from behind in order to sustain her until family arrived. Soon her mother was there, holding her hand, then her sister, and finally her father arrived. When her father assumed my place she was deep in a coma, her vital signs rapidly fading, gasping for breath in huge shudders. As an hour passed, we huddled about the bed, each person touching her, each of us weeping. Suddenly Janet opened her eyes and straightened her back. "What's the matter?" she asked. "I'm all right. I have been watching you all on television and it's all right."

As though it was the purpose of her almost magical awakening, she addressed each of us, assuring us of her love; then just as abruptly she again lapsed into coma. Within an hour she died. I felt no resigned grief, just love and wonder for a person who had managed to preside over her own death. You might even say she had returned from out of body just to reassure us. For from her words it seemed she had been witnessing the entire play of her death from a serene distance, "watching on television."

* * *

Amy's was a prolonged, exhausting struggle against death. And as the weeks passed she gathered me in for support until I was at her bed almost nightly, massaging her emaciated limbs and aching back, reading to her, holding her hand. For months she, too, had needed to be propped in bed to breathe. Her lungs had collapsed repeatedly, and she had even been dependent on mechanical ventilation for weeks at a time; but she refused to accept death, opposing it with all her will. She had no faith in God, did not presume that death was more than just a bitter annihilation. She had once been stunning to look at but her struggle with death had withered her. In heartrending gasps she recited fables of love and romance that she longed for. When she was hemorrhaging she pleaded for passages from the Bible to be read, but as soon as the episodes passed she was again immune to religion and its hopes.

I never doubted that Amy would survive the death process and be transformed, but she did not want to hear of it. She did not want to discuss death or the strict society of religion; she wanted to be granted the boon of healing and romance and wild happiness. And if she could not have that she just wanted to be supported and loved.

With Amy I was made aware of the importance of being just lovingly present—never bartering upon the subject of death or offering spurious hope of confirming her dreams—but just being a person who could be trusted, a person capable of enduring death with her and therefore remaining unrelentingly present. Amy's campaign against death never waned. With will of flint she sucked each breath from her collapsed lungs, her heart ever enlarging just to pump her blood, her arms and legs no more than flesh-lined bones.

When death claimed her I was exhausted, for her resolve, even in the day leading up to her death, never waned. She wanted to live. Months prior to this her husband had abandoned her and in the most heart-wrenching of scenes appeared an hour after she died to remove her jewelry—he was not working and was in need of cash to support his habits.

Her death was bitter, engaging, but it had not been a degradation, for Amy's strength was transmuted in me into a spiritual endurance, and we shared considerable love and happiness in those months. What Amy wanted most desperately was to love and be loved, which according to the harsh rigors of her experience was a matter of romance. She was loved because she was pleasant to look upon, which made it harder for her to release her grip on the image of her body. She presumed there was no love without it. But as death progressed she did not despise her husband or regret the beauty she had had to renounce; her splendid fire poured into the world. She made love with a mere glance or slight touch, all the coarse images of romance and desire seemingly burned up and replaced with a serene, heart-shattered romance with the entire world. And it was evidence to me that in death we all have a chance to become a spiritual alchemist.

I did not attend her funeral because I did not want to mourn her image; I wanted to recall her extreme perseverance against death and the opportunity it provided her to transmute her love. Death for her was not a leap, but a gradual passing through of barriers to reach that with which her heart was most aligned.

* * *

A third friend, Michael, had practically been raised in the hospital and, now grown, worked in our respiratory therapy department. He had married a Christian and had been born again, witnessing for Christ in the wards and converting a number of the patients with the same disease. He was a shining example that many in the hospital emulated. But then he renounced his faith and pointedly set upon a path of extremes. He became both a hard drinker and a talented poet. Eventually he resumed his spiritual quest in the realms of the occult and magical. When he needed surgeries and it was apparent that his decline had begun, Michael decided that he preferred death and the subject absorbed him. And even though his health was not severely compromised at first, he began deteriorating almost as an act of sheer will.

Though becoming more and more breathless, his state was not yet critical. His wife, though estranged from him and tormented that he was not a Christian, hovered near him, providing for him in a true Christian spirit even though between them there was a chasm destined never to be mended. Seeing them apart but in the same room, their marriage a bitter wound, was heartrending.

He was aware that I had helped with the death of his friends and though he was not requesting such help he was curious about what had transpired and what attracted me to this endeavor. He was enamored with the subjects of near-death and "astral travel" and repeatedly, though unsuccessfully, had attempted to induce such states, for he was searching for reassurance regarding death. Because of his need I confided in him that I had had many such travels and that they were not necessarily vital or spiritual. He summoned me frequently to his room to discuss my experiences and in return he laid bare his heart, worried that he should never have renounced Christ or looked into the magical arts. I suggested that he accept both, professing Christ as his saviour and looking forward to the magical realms across the bounds of death.

As his illness progressed he refused most medical treatment, as it just hampered his awareness and confined him to bed. His health waned in the next weeks; and just days before his death he expressed frustration that he had not glimpsed across the barrier of death. Yet he told me of a dream that was "strangely real." He dreamed that he was asleep in bed and then was ejected from his body, rising through the rooms of the hospital, even above the night, until he found himself in heaven where all about him were Christians feasting and celebrating. His heart sank, as this sight confirmed his regrets and fears. But then he rose further and toured a realm invisible to Christians, where Muslims and Jews and others were engaged in similar feasts. Michael related this dream to me with his usual fragile humor. And he was comforted when I affirmed what he suspected, that this dream was the "magic" for which he had been searching.

Chapter Twenty-Three

Abandoning Truth and Merging with Love

*A million samadhis can't launder the heart;
A billion experiences is not a journey,
but just the slime of a snail's path.
Open your arms wide and permit the Ganges
to flow through; love like a Gopi
and Krishna will sneak up behind
and gaze out of your eyes.*

The goal of my meditation became service, as I grew more committed to contributing my spare hours to patients. For it was plain that the patients entrusted to me were all my dependents, intricately linked to me, mirrors in which I was continuously appearing. And on nights off I went into town looking for the homeless, providing them with funds and helping them seek shelter.

My mind was not prattling on, nor were my energies dissipated on unhappiness or wonder. What I was struck by was that all human beings had an unquenchable desire for enlightenment and beauty, and it was no more important that I achieve it than they. All the world's motion was seeking the same rarified beauty. I concluded that there was no truth, no perfect mental pose that we were pursuing, for truth is spiritually inedible. At best truth is a dull pandering to the mind. What we are truly yearning for is transcendent beauty, and when we possess and are possessed by such splendor the concept of truth will wither away and never be heard from again. Enlightenment is so irresistible because of its beauty and we are transformed not because of truth, but because of the beauty and pleasure of a soul. This realization was a shock to me, for I had assumed that I had been diligently tracking truth across spiritual deserts.

When the flow of nature is not hardened into a self, then all that exists is a sacred realm. There is no mortal subject or embodied spirit; we are a maze of links and radiations that spread out in space, surrounding and presiding over the body—just as we are pearls of contracted awareness, that through internal pressure and energies are patterned like souls. What exists is not a self, but a choir of identities that speak out according to the context and mood. I jotted this down in my notes:

> Rebirth is generated by the need for latches upon awareness and partitions between experiences, so that many internal egos must be created to preside over this affair.

I share a resonance of spirit with my wife Loree, and she has provided support and critique that has induced me to examine more what I am providing to others with my spiritual venture. I am bound to my wife in exactly the same way that I am intricately linked and bound to all sentient beings. She is what I love in order to reach out to the rest of the world. Spirit shines through human possibilities not because an "individual" is transcendent but because the entire affair, each particle of it, is transcendent. There have been moments, even days, when it seemed that I was on the magical loom of the gods, but each of us remains in the company of his paradoxes and disharmonies regardless of what light we have bathed in. Despite it all we are just souls with homing instincts.

Loree is astute, more so than I. She is capable of rapidly assessing and memorizing experience and unlike most of us was never enraged that the world would not obey her. As a child, she never presumed, as most do, that the world was her personal magic. When just a girl she would ponder the nature of the universe, wondering how such an unlikely thing could exist—and the universe would summarily vanish and she would sink into a formless sky-like happiness. She picked up each meditation I exposed her to, rapidly mastering it, silencing her mind and drawing in the kundalini with equal dexterity. But she was not a spiritual dependent of mine; she was seeking illumination according to her own nature and calling. I would have discouraged her if I had not needed her, for the spiritual path can be bitter and arduous. Spiritual affairs hammer and belittle us until we submit. Yet there is an eloquence to it. Retracing my spiritual passage with Loree, it could be appreciated as a continuum, from her more sane and rational perspective.

Loree preferred Tibetan Buddhism and it was at her urging that I applied a careful reading to *The Tibetan Book of the Dead* and was able to untangle my death experiences. Loree and I went to hear the Dalai Lama speak, even though I had not attended a spiritual retreat or conference in more than a decade. (I had once obtained tickets to hear Krishnamurti speak at Carnegie Hall, but decided against it at the last minute, deciding to remain apart from all that was formal and organized.) We met the Dalai Lama outside his hotel and, oddly, the next morning we showed up on the front page of the morning paper next to him.

We utilize our vacations as spiritual pilgrimages, choosing places conducive to meditation. It was during these vacations that many new developments sprang up. During one, it occurred to me that I was addicted to concepts of the spiritual.

We mapped out a vacation in the spring of 1993 so that we would visit a Hindu shrine in West Virginia and the Museum of Tibetan Arts in New York City, go to a Franciscan monastery in Washington, and travel on to Assateague Island in the Chesapeake Bay. It was on Assateague that the flaw in my spiritual approach was revealed: I depended too much on concepts and that to be acutely spiritual we must be recreated as a lover, a resonating chamber for the spirit, much like Krishna's flute. I had kept journals tracking spiritual themes and this visit inspired me to return to poetry, to drawing and painting.

We were setting out in the morning toward the bridge to the island when it overwhelmed me that there was no concept that could translate the absolute and that all my analyzing had just worked to mark and divide, creating premises which ensnared meditation. My ego was subtly holding onto my meditation through the process of attempting to conceptualize that which can never be held in mind. I was gazing through the windshield at the sunlit clouds over Assateague when all concepts regarding the Divine just vanished. And it was wordlessly apparent that the conceptual mind could never touch upon a significant realization. When we awaken to the divine we also awaken from the parade of concepts and theories that work in conjunction with reality but never explain. To meditate is to penetrate the wake of a moving universe but it does not explain or justify what is discovered there. We can contact light but we cannot grasp or order it—the supreme is never achieved; we must just move or dance with it. But I still held onto a subtle doubt, and so I asked for a sign that this was the right course—perhaps a foolish response, but the irrationality of it suddenly appealed to me.

Combing the beach at dusk that same day, I described to Loree my experience of relaxing my grasp of the conceptual, seeing it then as part of the process of unfolding within the domains of the spiritual. Then I mentioned to her that on all the beaches I had ever visited I had never happened across a chambered shell, such as a conch, and that it was probably too late in the evening, that the beach would have been picked over. In just a few strides a large chambered nautilus shell washed up at my feet. Within a couple of steps more a second shell emerged from the breakers and within reach of that a third. Folks were milling nearby in the surf, but not a single person

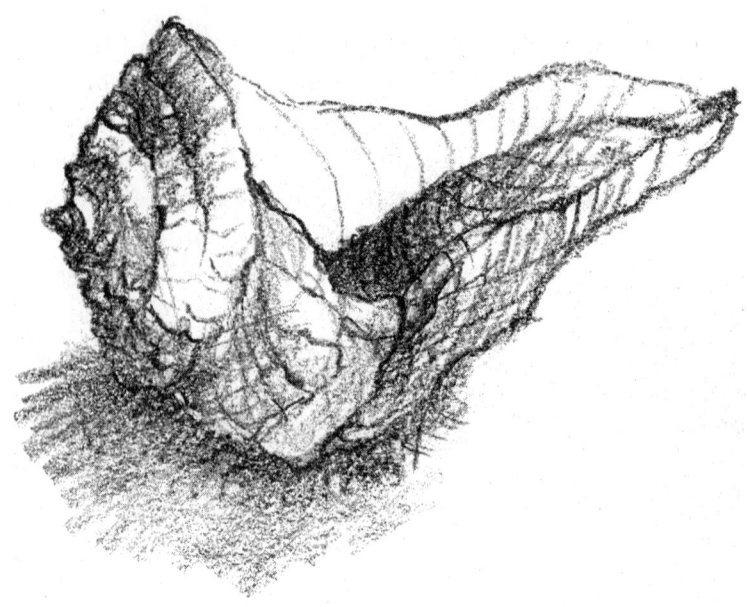

seemed to have noticed the shells. Quickly we picked them up and, although it was not a miracle, I assumed that it was the sign I had asked for. If we cannot step outside the spirit, then neither can we examine it or subjugate it to our reason. We must be reasonable, but to oversupport the conceptual mind is to dismember the divine.

On the trip home we stopped in southern Ohio at a park carved by the ages into magical ravines, streams, and yawning caves. Here I began to hear a resonance like muted thunder, which was the breathless Om of the *Upanishads*. Gradually the forest about me became drenched in this hum, communing with the primal cause. I had encountered it once in its most potent form in a near-death experience. It had been a rising thunder upon which the soul had been transported: a raga of death and rebirth. That day in the park with Loree it was just an uninhibited pleasure that I did not attempt to interpret, permitting the Om to appear and express itself unhindered. Neither did I mourn it when it vanished.

After we returned home, I was strolling in the yard when the Om resonated again. As it did so a point of indescribably beautiful light approached me from over the trees. As the light merged with my heart I realized that it had been my soul reflected outside myself. A sign of a transformation that had occurred that week at the level of the heart.

My health continued to improve, as I was healed from the stress I had placed on myself in the years of spiritual seeking, mixed with bouts of indulgence and depression. We bought a home and I exercised, gardened, no longer pondering my death experiences. I had finally realized that death is just a process by which we are all taken apart and rearranged. We are bound to be tested by death, but we are transfigured according to immutable laws, not annihilated or punished or even rewarded. But we cannot merge at death if it is not our habit to exist in mutual interdependence, merging with all experience, even the most mundane. Interdependence was just a technical Buddhist expression for love, or an embrace that is not abstract, but a present and ongoing process. Buddha's wish was simply to remain beneath his pipal tree, to bask in the enlightenment that he had so arduously won. It was his love that set him on a path of preaching in India along roads more treacherous than we can presently imagine. The entire form of his life was a sacrifice of love. When he taught the doctrines of impermanence and bare attention, what he was transmitting was that we must love in this moment, this moment, and this. Presently, persistently and infinitely. It was just that simple.

Death is in the present, the bardos after death are in the present, even birth is in the present; if we remain in the present we are on an unshakable foundation. And that foundation is love. It is just that simple.

> Both the dream and the previous night's sleep
> And the realization of its unreality when you
>   awake
> Are one in the nature of illusion.
> Take this as the bardo of the dream.
> —Gampopa[12]

Chapter Twenty-Four

At Rest in Awakening

*We should not march our
spirits but usher them
in singing and dancing,
reposing in all sixteen
of Kali's arms like
a lover.*

One night I was lying in bed in the spare bedroom because I had not been able to sleep. When I finally did manage to get to sleep I awakened in just an hour, making a trip to the kitchen. As I returned to bed, an inexplicable rage swept over me. I paced the house attempting to calm this fury, storming past the bedroom where Loree was sleeping. She awoke but I did not respond to her inquiries and instead climbed back into bed. As I was adjusting the sheets I noticed a tingling numbness in my legs, and my heart was racing. I struggled to maintain my composure, as it had the familiar texture of a death experience.

Suddenly Loree and I were browsing in a gray, fading general store, though the shelves were bare except for a small rack of sale items upon a limping wooden cart near the cash register.

My wife was intent upon examining each of these objects and I was seated on a wooden chair ignoring them. Finally she was won over by a small, framed picture that she brought over to show me. The background was mirrored and on the gleaming surface was the portrait of a male figure with his hair in a top-knot. I glanced at it and nodded, then impatiently returned to my brooding.

Then the clerk breezed in. I barely glanced at him as he began extolling the virtues of the items on his sales cart.

"These objects are of inestimable value," he assured me. "Please look at them. Only two dollars," he groaned as he retrieved an item from the bottom shelf, presenting me with a small, white stupa.

I was quite impressed, but when I looked up, gesturing as if to pay, he had vanished.

Then I awoke. Scattering the sheets, I stood alongside my bed, not noticing until then that the stupa was still in my care, transferred to me during the dream. I stumbled across the hall and sat down on the floor by Loree's bed, shouting for her to awaken. "Look at this! Look what I found in my dream."

She seemed to be resisting, as though reluctant to join me. When she finally did turn over and look at what I was holding, the stupa began crumbling, reduced to ash. Revealed within the ash was the bust of a sacred figure, the likes of which I had never seen. I returned to my room cradling the figure and placed it on the shelf in the corner. As I did so, many sacred artifacts began appearing all about it on the shelf, as though manifested by the bust. Their intensity was almost overwhelming to behold and I stepped back, attempting to hold onto my awareness, which seemed intent on slipping away.

Among the precious objects were some that were primitive and blackly opaque. But there were also intricate Buddhist figures, richly filigreed and ornamented. The shelves were a shrine of icons and images of such eminent force that I could barely look at them. Nestled among the spiritual talismans was an inscribed plaque that I could not read. Within the frame was a certificate of my own spiritual attainment—upon it a list of previous births. Yet I distrusted it as well, as its appeal was to my vanity. I was convinced then that I was trapped in an after-death state and perhaps actually dying.

I stood very straight before this altar of images and clapped my hands three times above my head, repeating each time, "I bow to the formless absolute." Then I relaxed into the formlessness.

As soon as this was done I awoke in bed. (Had I not already awakened?) I climbed out of bed, aware that I was still enmeshed in the death process, for the scene was too intense and too readily malleable. I went to my wife's room to appeal for help but in her stead there was another woman, whom upon closer look I realized was not even human. Her gaze was too penetrating, her mouth was sensuous and red with human blood.

I was aware that I must act, that my liberation depended upon my sense of purpose and so returned to my room, standing at the foot of the bed and facing west. I clapped my hands over my head again three times and repeated that I surrendered myself to the formless absolute. As I did so, a blazing light descended upon me. Fleetingly there were sparks rushing about me, as though I was near a furnace, and then I was overwhelmed with light—light that was so intense that it was almost too much to bear and I had to strain to steady myself and not collapse. Then I was submerged in darkness.

When I awoke no more than a few minutes had passed; the residue of the experience was palpable in the air in the room. I had no doubt that it was a brief encounter with a bardo, but my responses surprised me. What had prompted me to clap my hands in such a manner and recite that phrase? Had I succeeded in cutting short or looking past death's illusions? For if I had read the bardos correctly in the Tibetan texts, it is a period of being saturated with our own unconscious dreams and cravings. If we do not "wake up" from the process then we are passed over to rebirth without a sense of having retreated to subtler realms and we even faint amid the ruins of our memory, sleeping until we are reborn. I lay in bed reflecting upon the metaphysical puzzle I had encountered. Finally I had encountered the bardo in its raw, most tangible form and I was now able to see it reflected in the Tantric and shamanistic traditions I had read about. I had experienced the desire to faint and the urge to resist the pure light when it descended into my dream. When the texts explain that most souls prefer the muted lights of rebirth, it is not a metaphorical statement as I had assumed.

I was literally reeling from the significance of all this when my wife rushed into my room to relate a dream from which she had just awakened. She dreamed that she had been showing an unknown friend a photograph of a monastery she had either recently visited or was planning to visit, a site that would be of great significance to her. As they were examining the image, the monastery transformed itself into an ordinary house of two stories.

As she examined the photograph further she found herself within its frame, actually walking up the drive toward the back of the house. As she rounded the corner into the yard, she happened upon a small swimming pool in which a male figure was immersed to his upper chest. His skin was a gleaming silver and he was bald except for a knotted turquoise and scarlet headdress. But her gaze was held by the man as he beckoned her into the pool, an invitation which she at first refused. But he persisted and she was drawn, as though magnetized, into the pool, bathing with him. At his suggestion, Loree began scooping water over her arms, at which point she took on the same silver tone as he.

According to the evidence, we seemed to be passing through modes of the same experiences, but she was surrendering to the form of a God while I was surrendering to a formless absolute—both of which, according to the ancient prophets of near-death and threshold events, could serve to clarify and untangle. And perhaps after repeated flirtations I had actually found wisdom relative to this transition. But then, I am no doubt speculating too much, presuming too much, for the death process is as unstable as gunpowder. Life proceeds into death so that the quality of life is that of death, though this is a matter we refuse to meet with or speak of while we are alive.

After this I would lapse into states where I was just awake, a raw wakefulness or awareness that contained no inherent splits or noticeable discord. I was not being translated into an expanded awareness, but was just being absorbed into my most primal, unconditional presence, just resting in the present. What was most fascinating about the experience was the "linking"; it was as though I was intimately linked with whatever I encountered—there was a constant upwelling of empathy. I loved.

I was not receding into a spiritual ocean as I had assumed, but stepping forward and reaching deeper into the mundane and chaotic; but unlike my prior awakening leading up to the events at Shakertown, this was rooted in the ineffable. These episodes addressed all that was spiritual and questing in me as the grand experiences of light and transcendence never had.

During a storm in the spring of 1994, the week before Easter, it suddenly occurred to me that we were all upon the same path. All spiritual pursuits seek to heal the rift that appears to divide reality into parts and whether we attain and submit to incandescent light, or Jesus, or no-self, or an indescribable bliss, or spheres of rarified being, or we have raised kundalini or been mindful to the point of nirvana, all that is actually happening is that we are communing with a vast field of being that includes all births and all that is too subtle to be born with a physical nature. We are all mirrors and mirror-images if we just appreciate that no ascent or sainthood is as effective as just relaxing into reality. It is a humble, quiet, all-consuming wisdom, easier to approach when we are purged of all that is wondrous and notable.

Each approach to enlightenment assumes a particular shape according to what has been lived, but it is all a divine embrace, an interdependence, a sharing: love. To be enlightened is to love, is to presume an indestructible affinity for all that we meet and are met with.

I tested this concept, resurrecting all the "enlightenments" I once experienced, assuming them for a week, testing them against the flood of events in hospital wards. I practiced meditating on consciousness as space, then as emptiness, then I expanded out into formless radiance. I meditated upon kundalini and raised the energies up the spine, recreating passages and forces. But along with all this I attempted to remain just present, an undivided representative of the reality in which all of this was occurring. There was no perpetual foundation, or self, no graspable entity that was the same in the past and future; but there was a transition of energies from moment to moment that was the stable heart of being.

But though each meditative state was initially pleasurable and fathomless, it soon grew stale, for a fresh approach was needed to again merge with the real. Any mere meditative state has to be perpetuated, argued, resurrected, or deepened; only love is an unalloyed meeting with the present.

By chance, in the summer of 1994, the story of Father Thomas received a footnote. Loree and I were driving with my parents through a summer's evening. My father was recovering from surgery and was in a somber mood as he provided me with directions. We swung down the road bordering the hill upon which the seminary of Father Thomas was perched. As we approached the field where it had once stood, my father explained that the Shaker barn, the last remnant of their heritage in the area, had burned down.

On a whim I turned into the seminary. His mood noticeably lightening, my father recalled that he often played there as a child. I was stunned, half because my father had never mentioned it before and half because he had been raised twenty miles away near Wright Patterson Air Force Base. He told me a relative of his had been a monk here, and when his parents paid visits he would be permitted to roam the fields and play.

As we drove past a cemetery of plain-hewn white stones on the side of a hill, my mother mentioned that it was restricted to nuns and priests. Perhaps my relative was resting there, perhaps near to Father Thomas. Considering the decades they inhabited perhaps they were acquainted; at the least he was likely familiar with the legends of Father Thomas. Perhaps the nun with whom I shared stories was interred there as well. As I looked at the seminary, the past mumbled into the present; so much was different and so much of what I had experienced was more suited to dreams than the report of the senses.

The same month, I heard rumors from a friend that there had been sightings of the Madonna stepping down from her niche in the stones. Reportedly she has touched the surface of the water in the stone basin next to the altar, bestowing upon it healing properties. But by then I was no longer interested in miracles, nor was I seeking a perfect image among the infinite appearances of reality. Rather, I was content to rest in reality and permit myself to be full of whatever is present. I was not seeking or pursuing reality; I was resting in it.

I wrote then:

We do not find the mystery with our awareness; our awareness is the mystery—just as it is.

Chapter Twenty-Five

Toward Simplicity: A Final Pilgrimage

I relax into the great mandala;
I breathe the sacred wheel.
My house is made of fire
and eternal wakefulness.
Love is my only song.
It has been a noble path
over seas, across mountains
Buddha's breath on
the candle of my self.

Glimpsing the soul is remarkably like seeing the morning star, which, according to the shaman Black Elk, is a sign of regeneration and wisdom. The same beacon of the dawn initiated realization in the Buddha, when he just looked up, glanced across the horizon at the morning star, and spontaneously awoke from the dream of manifest existence. Even the song of Lauds, in the Christian church, praises the morning star.

By the summer of 1994, the rich, sparkling blue drop of meditation had grown more lucent and ethereally white in appearance. But by then it was plain that this radiance was just a marker, of less significance than the daybreak star because it could not be conjured each successive dawn and shared.

All the experiences I had ever had were just markers, pointers, like the eastern star huddling upon the horizon. The garden in my yard is just as much a spiritual event as arousing the kundalini or a passage into death. If we presume too much, conjecture too much, then spiritual experiences are just a fetish, a ritualized disruption. As we become more illuminated we bury what was spiritual and restructuring in favor of what is mundane and natural; not that we have abandoned the spiritual, just that the spirit is spread out over the earth. We are not all patterned to arouse kundalini or look past the entropy of death or sink the mind into a vacuum of nonexperience, but we are all entitled to assume the most enduring aspect of reality—wakefulness. I had no myth at my human core; my walking rapture was just to be present, to arise and re-arise continuously.

My role at the hospital expanded and I was permitted to work in newborn intensive care, staff a birthing ward, and perform sleep studies. Since the age of thirty, each plunge into the current of the hospital was a test for what I had found in my spiritual oasis and had to be translated back into rigid, hard experience. Many spiritual gains thought to be indestructible were broken when I was summoned to "codes" in the emergency room. During crucial ambulance transports, it was just the nurse and I who were expected to manage and implement care; stress was pumped into my veins almost nightly. A meditation that could not withstand the raw grievances of experience would not do. There was a time when I assumed my career in the hospital was hampering my progress, but it was now apparent that it provided me with a chaffing of my meditation practices. Wisdom could not be an abstraction, but must be tested in the most extreme circumstances, with compassion as its handmaiden.

I had dreamed of basking on sunbaked rocks along the sea, my most enduring dream, or of retreating to a cave to harvest my spirit in peace. I would have liked to be a hermit. But it was my fortune to be in a hospital among the corrosive winds of human suffering. I could not afford to water down my senses or humor a vacant bliss. The hospital is where death is repeatedly enacted—the actual horizon of the sacred, which shrines just pretend to inhabit.

Late that autumn Loree and I traveled to England to visit churches and pagan sites—the visit almost an act of homage to Father Thomas. Our route was across southern and western England, then Wales, into Cornwall, Glastonbury, Salisbury, and Land's End, the thread of it the ancient legends and seers.

It was while upon this pleasant journey that wakefulness, which I then was terming as "mere presence" was released. I alone was not primordially awake; all that I could see, hear, notice, or find was just as awake. The "seeing" I practiced intuitively as a child had finally achieved its most simple and complete expression. When I looked at an object, even casually, it was not just present, but present as indestructible awareness, even if it was apparently inanimate. But this awareness did not depend on a witnessing aspect; there was no inner and outer in this presence, and form and formless were so perfectly matched and absorbed that there was no trace of either—just conscious presence.

This consummate state is the most simple and vital, what we are always living but cannot see. We cannot examine or dissect this presence; we can only become it. Whereas before I possessed techniques for making me aware, now it was impossible not to be. I had no existence or form apart from awareness. Awareness was just as apparent to me as the tip of a hair, a stone, the blue pearl, or inner soul. There was no need to meditate; I needed to only relax into what is most vital and real about each experience.

When we were at Land's End, on a rugged coast with a foaming ocean beneath and foaming clouds above us, enjoying a picnic lunch, the most hidden aspect of this meditation suddenly appeared to me. I was not constrained in this awareness as a witness. The witness is the most rudimentary form of self; the ego can be maintained as a reference point and a prop for experience, but without a witness it has no inherent existence. It is the very act of being within a form, witnessing in accord with senses and minds, that prevents us from birth from realizing that awareness is all-consuming. This was the sum of my realization; I was not a witness, or shape within awareness, but just an awareness independent of any interior or soul-like reference. I was, without recourse or resort, just absurdly human, neither a sage nor a saint. Once the witness vanished, the last support had been removed and awareness shone through all that I encountered.

From this event arose a meditation that is a perfect expression of this awakening. Because the witness is a fixed way of seeing, all that is needed to rest in unalloyed presence is just to relax the witness's hold on awareness. This meditation practice enables us to realize that it is the witness that sets us apart from the flow of reality. All meditations work with awareness, but this meditation addresses it directly. We must liberate awareness by seeing that it is not located within and does not exist separately as a witness. To do so is to realize there is no inner awareness, that awareness is most fundamentally shapeless and boundless.

We begin this meditation by noticing whether or not we are holding awareness within our body. We must then relax so profoundly that awareness does not seem to be held within, but is an unbounded space. What is most vital is not the content or nature of awareness but its location, so that we may inquire, "Where is awareness?" and then relax as deeply as we can from the inside out. We must then remain relaxed in this field of diffuse awareness without altering or judging our state. Very likely the witness will repeatedly return to its seat within the body, so we must ask ourselves again and again, "Where is awareness?" and again relax deeply from within to without. It is this unconscious reflex to return to a fixed point of awareness within which, with continued practice, we eventually learn to spontaneously relax. If we continue to inquire and relax, we will even-

tually transcend our body and gradually find that our hold on awareness has been at the root of our suffering. In response, awareness will abide more around than within, arising with all that *Is*. The practice is perfect and perfectly simple because it does not work with what is within consciousness, but with where and what consciousness is. (This meditation is expanded upon in the Afterword.)

We headed north again, across the moors at night, alighting at the border of Wales and England among rugged hills and squat mountains. Here it seemed as though I was completing the long search that had not made me either refined or virtuous, but had bestowed happiness. I was neither spiritual nor non-spiritual, and it seemed that I could not even claim to have attained or not attained; I was just an emanation of awareness, an hallucination in a moment of conscious being. I was reminded of a passage from the *Lankavatara Sutra*, here paraphrased, which once had made no sense to me:

> Enlightenment has no definite form or nature by which it can manifest itself, so in enlightenment itself, there can be no thing to be enlightened. Enlightenment exists solely because of our delusions, and if they disappear so will enlightenment. And the opposite is also true, there are no delusions apart from enlightenment. No thing exists that is not a form of enlightenment. But we must also be careful not to presume that enlightenment is a mere "thing" that can be grasped, or it too will become an impediment. When the mind that was deluded finally becomes enlightened, it passes away, and with its passing, the thing which we have referred to as enlightenment passes also.

That night I playfully composed a doctrine that was a no-doctrine, an enlightenment whose gates I imagined admitted no sages and saints, but was populated with the rustic folk I saw in the pastures of western Wales.

— We either believe or don't believe awareness is primary to all existence. If we don't believe then religion and the spiritual has no home for us. If we do believe we must just trust and be aware of whatever appears, just as it appears, trusting implicitly that it is the same awareness.
— Awareness is never excluded, but is hidden among the realms of experience, so that it just seems to magically materialize, even evoking subtle aspects. But it has always remained perfectly present.
— There is no path to realization; we must just relax into the present, trusting in its spiritual depth.
— There is no evidence of this realization except the willingness to love.

We are never apart from God or death or transcendence or error. Despite all I had sacrificed in my journey toward enlightenment, I had never actually departed. Yet I arrived into the awareness I had always been resting upon but ignoring. The ladder to the heart I had been searching for since childhood had been before me all along.

To approach awareness we must not even accept such terms as attainment and nonattainment, or self and no-self, or continuity or its lack. If we partition existence or cling to any dualism, then mere presence will elude us. To be awake is to be at rest within the matrix of experiences. A person thusly awake is not exalted or made perfect; he or she is just made robustly human and calmly imperfect, but awake.

As the Zen sutra has said:

> For many years I dug the ground looking for blue sky,
> accumulating layers and layers of mediocrity.
> One night in the darkness, the roof tiles were blown away.
> The bones of emptiness dissolved of themselves.[13]

Returning home, I was again unremarkable, neither particularly gifted nor radiant. I am a husband, dedicated to this project of marriage. And in my work I am a care-giver, having acknowledged that my purpose is to work beyond the physical realm of the hospital, to help the soul transcend from the physical to the ephemeral; in the process, to help the human being on the human level understand, to feel, and to accept that transition.

The wisdom of presence is perennial, but it is expressed just as an honorable heart. My human decline has begun, but I am without regrets, implacably present and graced. In all and always I am sharing the source of love, for sharing is all that I am capable of or fit for. I am no longer intoxicated by my own mind or by my inner tale and narrations, for as rough and unpleasant as it is, I am the world—I *must* be compassionate.

As silent as Patanjali;
the unforgettable dawn of Atman;
the glow unbinding form;
a jewel in the heart cave;
the untamable Goddess;
all a long journey
returning to the Self.

No secrets, no refuge, no treasures,
no lakelike voids or karma streams.
Just the thunderous song
of Awakening
with no root or flower.

Afterword

The Practice of Inquiry

The light that sees is the eternal light,
and the seemingly unattainable horizon
is ever beneath our steps.

To ask of ourselves "where is awareness" is to look at that which is inside all that is. There are bones of light, there are physical bodies and minds that seem to be housed within these bodies, but within this within, behind it all, is awareness. We are always watching impassively even as we think we are chasing after dreams and pleasures. We are only apparently chasing after our dreams and sense hallucinations; inwardly we are always just watching. All that we are presently seeing is chemically dreamed up by the mind; the mind is a lens which is directing awareness. Beneath what the mind is projecting is just a sea of light, an exhilarating dance of light and love. Yet awareness is the inner part of this as well. So just to be fully aware is not to have solved all the riddles of life but to have slipped out of them, so that all that remains is this light that is our awakened nature, ever sleepless, ever shining. To ask "where is awareness" is to see that this awareness is within all we experience; but never is it hidden. It is even the source of all light and life. And love.

What is striking and wonderful about this awareness is that it is a state that is not separate from the rest of existence. So to ask where it is is not to search for it per se, but just to realize that our awareness is within all that exists. This "within" is not hidden, but all that we can meet with or take apart is equally "inside." There is no outside to life; all that we experience is perfectly inside awareness, just as it appears, without need to subtly examine it or simplify it. For our awakeness is not reducible to a mere state—it is the life of all that is. And when we finally realize that this incessant awakeness is at the heart of life, we have engaged in loving. We have no work except to guide all who are presently sleeping within their own selves to this perfect awareness and love.

In life we continually relay stories to our minds and at death these stories will visibly arise and overwhelm us. But if we have practiced returning the mind to its inner self, or the ground of awareness, then at death it will inevitably arise in mind "where is awareness" and we will begin to restore ourselves to our naked simplicity. By virtue of its utter simplicity our awareness then can remove the veils of our illusions. And our liberation will be imminent. We will be returned to ground or our minds which is even the self of light—and the only agent of love in all the realms of birth and death.

But beneath all this is a hidden law, which simply states that if we are loved by a being who dwells within awareness in our behalf, again our liberation from death's trials will be imminent. This much I have learned about the process of life and death. The transition into life and death is entirely dependent on love. Love leads irrevocably back to a deathless awakening, not to a mindless return to a gross form. Love overreaches all form and is the liberation that is readily available to all of us. Death is a process; there is no exact moment of death except by our biological accounting, so we have many, many chances to see through it to the divine gaze of love.

To inquire as to where awareness is, is also to put us directly in the path of love, for only love and our conscious nature have no home and so must abide in all places at once. We are liberated when we have so profoundly relaxed the self and all separating motives that we too have no particular home, so must accept all that appears as our home and love it just as dearly as our most intimate lover. This, and not mere concepts and meditative practices, is the heart and fire of liberation.

When repeatedly asked about the nature of liberation, the Buddha stubbornly refused to answer. He could not answer really, for liberation is the inside of all outsides and so can never be separated out and inspected, can never be pointed at directly and exclusively. The state of liberation is the watcher watching himself and the lover loving himself and meeting himself in a thousand thousand different disguises. Mere form cannot fool our awakened nature from just seeing that all appearances are just a play upon awareness.

The flow of events that carries us through our lives is not an independent reality, but a projection of our mind. In essence, we are perpetually meditating on a physically induced hallucination; it is not occurring in a particular place and has no reason for being here. There is no "here" apart from awareness. Just ask of awareness with a slight persistence and it will begin to reveal its nature. The mind continually forgets that what is appearing is just being projected from within upon a wordless sea of light. To inquire as I have suggested is just to remind it and by simply doing so also restore us to our love, so that in life and death our energies are liberated from their selfish patterns and habits, our afterlife radiated with awareness.

If we seek liberation selfishly and not as an act of love, then it will become a meditative trick and will not support us in life and especially after death. The purpose of meditation is not to attain liberation just for our self but for all, to love fully and irrevocably. If we do not love, then we rise only to plummet back to ourselves at death. But if we return our minds to its underlying awareness, then our death becomes an alchemical transformation that tangibly assists every person we have ever loved. We walk on a homeless, groundless awakening that intricately binds us to all that is, and with such a realization passing over the threshold of death is barely noticed. Within the process of awakening we will each find our inner calling, a calling that has set aside the story of our lives in order to assist in the way in which we are most gifted. Our story then is an outgrowth of spiritual work and has no inherent purpose apart from service and love—this is the nature of liberation.

> *The heart is thirsting.*
> *And we seek to quench it with treasures;*
> *But we cannot drink our fill*
> *except from colorless waters;*
> *And not till all the treasures we have gathered*
> *have been returned to stone.*
> *Carrying no-mind, no-God,*
> *no-dream, imagine that there is*
> *no imagination. And see. That all*
> *scriptures and icons exist*
> *within the diamond of love.*

Notes

1. Arthur Osborne, *Ramana Maharshi and the Path of Self Knowledge* (New York: Samuel Weiser, Inc., 1970), pp. 18-19.

2. Jiddu Krishnamurti, *The Flight of the Eagle* (New York: Harper and Row, 1971), pp. 31-32.

3. Jiddu Krishnamurti, *Meditations* (New York: Harper and Row, 1979), p. 1.

4. Thomas Cleary, trans., *Rational Zen: The Mind of Dogen Zenji* (Boston: Shambhala Press, 1992), p. 43.

5. Osborne, *Ramana Maharshi and the Path of Self Knowledge*, pp. 176-177.

6. V.K. Seth, *Kabir: The Weaver of God's Name* (Punjab, India: Radha Soami Satsang Beas, 1984), p. 607.

7. Osborne, *Ramana Maharshi and the Path of Self Knowledge*, p. 20.

8. Osborne, *Ramana Maharshi and the Path of Self Knowledge*, pp. 149-150.

9. Linda Hess and Shukdev Singh, trans., *A Touch of Grace* (Boston: Shambhala Press, 1994), p. 119.

10. Coleman Barks, trans., *Essential Rumi* (San Francisco, HarperSanFrancisco, 1995), p. 281.

11. Osborne, *Ramana Maharshi and the Path of Self Knowledge*, p. 78.

12. The Nalanda Committee, trans., *The Rain of Wisdom* (Boston: Shambhala, 1980), p. 238.

13. Kazuaki Tanahashi and Tensho David Snyder, trans., *Essential Zen* (San Francisco: HarperSanFrancisco, 1994), p. 76.

Glossary

Bardo: From the Tibetan, literally translated as "in-between state"; concept referring particularly to the state that lies between death and rebirth. According to this tradition there is a forty-nine day lapse in the ordinary process of death and birth when the mind is absorbed in its own hallucinations and dreams, a process that leads to rebirth and regaining of a physical form. The supreme light "dawns" occasionally during this state and so it is considered by the Tibetan tradition as a ripe occasion for being delivered from the rounds of rebirth. *The Tibetan Book of the Dead* or, as it actually is titled, *The Bardo Thödol* (meaning "Liberation through Hearing in the In-between State") is read over the body of the recently deceased. If he is not capable of realizing the supreme light then at least he is supposedly helped in receiving a favorable rebirth.

Bindu: From the Sanskrit, *bindu* can be translated as "a particle or spot," which can appear during deep meditation as extremely small and bright points of light. A bindu is an unmanifest source of power. According to the system of kundalini yoga, there are bindus, or seeds, within the middle of each chakra. These bindus are often referred to as human "souls" and are bridges between the Absolute and personal existence.

Chakra: The term *chakra* refers to a "wheel," but is frequently described as a lotus. It is within the system of chakras that the spiritual energies unfold. The chakras are related to but not the same as various glands and nerve plexuses throughout the body. Each chakra is depicted with a certain number of petals, which can be awakened or unfurled with a guru's blessings, mantras, mandalas, and various meditation practices. Each chakra has a particular spiritual function and significance, each a vortex through which spiritual energies reach into the world. Once the transformation has begun it is irrevocable, the process spontaneously manifesting over days and years.

According to Hindu doctrine there are six chakras located within the physical form, the seventh transcending all physical existence and located above the crown of the head. The *muladhara-chakra* is at the perineum and is associated with the downward movement of vital energies unless the *kundalini-shakti* is awakened; the *svadhishthana-chakra* is at the genitals and is where the ego is rooted; the *manipura-chakra* is at the naval and is connected with the upward movement of vital energies; the *anahata-chakra* is at the heart and it is from here that the subtle, spiritual music arises; the *vishuddha-chakra* is at the throat and is the chakra of inspiration and creativity; between and behind the eyes is the *ajna-chakra*, or what is frequently referred to as the "third eye." This is the site of infinite mind and where the reflection of the Absolute occurs in the human body; the *sahdasrara-chakra*, or "thousand-spoked wheel" is above the head. It is at this seventh chakra that human consciousness meets with unspeakable radiance of the Absolute. When this infinite light is met, what is referred to as *nirvakalpa samadhi* is experienced.

Jnana samadhi: An utterly formless absorption in which consciousness is merged with itself. Consciousness in this state is utterly without content; there is no world or outer awareness, not even a sense of emptiness. *Jnana* is derived from the Sanskrit root, "to know." The practice of Jnana is considered among the four fundamental yogas of India.

Krishna: The most celebrated of all Hindu Gods, Krishna's name indicates that he was black or dark blue in color. He is the hero of the *Bhagavad Gita*, the most popular of all Hindu scriptures. Krishna became an object of considerable personal devotion, a devotion that later developed into a fourth limb of yoga, *bhakti yoga*—the yoga of love. Bhakti is a practice that seeks unification with the Divine through personal love.

Kundalini: The term *kundalini* refers to the serpent power that is usually dormant, or coiled up at the base of the spine. Once aroused from its slumber, its energies are magnified and it seems to rise up the spine, piercing the subtle centers, or chakras. Because it houses the kundalini, the human form is a map of the spiritual universe, spontaneously bestowing upon a person as it rises various powers and experiences. When the energy reaches the summit of its movement, *samadhi*, or spiritual absorption, occurs in which the mind is as "brilliant as a million suns."

Mandala: A tool of meditation that is looked upon as a representation of the spiritual universe; an image that is usually circular, but always self enclosed. The center point of a mandala is often referred to as a seed, or *bindu*, the point of concentration of forces that is the link between the manifest and unmanifest worlds. In Tibetan Buddhism there are complex, pictorial mandalas that house deities with which one can merge through visualization practices.

Out-of-Body Travel: Out-of-body or *astral* travel occurs during dreams, during severe states of mental upheaval, and after death. The astral, or subtle body, is composed of *prana*, which can be seen as the aura around the physical form.

Prana: The word *prana* indicates breath, or more accurately "the inner breath," in which the energies of *kundalini-shakti* are at play. Prana is not the mere physical breath, but an indestructible life breath that links us with the Absolute.

Ram: In the Hindu pantheon, Ram was an incarnation of Vishnu. Ram and his wife are viewed by Hindus as the perfect spiritual coupling, and he is venerated as a divine incarnation that was both spiritually enlightened and active in the world.

Roshi: A venerable master in the Zen tradition. Training in the art of Zen takes place under such a master, who can be an ordained or lay member of the community. Such a teaching obligation depends solely upon the enlightenment of the roshi himself.

Samadhi: Translated as "to establish, or make firm," samadhi is absorption in a state outside the usual rounds of sleep, dream, and waking consciousness. In samadhi the subject merges with the object of concentration. There are gradients of samadhi, the highest of which is considered *nirvakalpa samadhi*, when the object of concentration is the radiant Absolute upon which all else depends.

Sanyasin: In the Hindu tradition, a person who has renounced the world and is wandering homeless in search of realization of God. He admits to no possessions and no attachments and depends utterly upon charity. Ramana Maharshi was such a figure.

Shabd: *Shabd* can be translated simply as "sound." It is the link between the motionless Absolute and the Shakti, or energy of creation. There is an inner or hidden aspect, which is vibration. The shabd can be heard within as innumerable forms of music and natural sound. But in its most potent form it is *Om*, which is similar in nature to thunder and in deep meditation is accompanied by profound vibrations that ascend through the body. On the crest of Om we are carried out of body and into spiritual realms. This practice is at the heart of what is referred to as *Kriya Yoga* in many traditions and essentially is a meditation that requires "conscious death." Shabd is the unstruck sound or the sound that is not created by the clashing of objects, but arises spontaneously from the unmanifest Absolute.

Shakti: *Shakti* can be translated as "spiritual energy" supporting the various worlds. In traditional Hindu lore this is personalized as the work of a goddess that is the consort of the Absolute, or Shiva, that stands outside the worlds. According to the Hindu tradition, the grace of the Goddess, or its Shakti, permits the worshiper to realize his supreme Self, for his Self is the same as that as Shiva/Shakti, or the play of the divine. Shakti is the energy that is roused when the kundalini awakens from its slumber.

Shaman: In ancient cultures, a person who was a representation of the tribe's entire spiritual matrix, acting in the roles of healer, priest, and magician. Such figures are usually looked upon as adepts in the practice of out-of-body travel, which is done in order to fulfill the various roles within their tribe.

Siddhi: In the Indian tradition, a spiritual master who is enlightened and who is often described as possessing extraordinary spiritual powers.

Sikhism: A religion, founded by Guru Nanak in northern India late in the Middle Ages, that seeks to meld the teachings of Hinduism and Islam.

Sufism: An undercurrent to Islam that seeks salvation through personal, uninhibited love of Allah. Influenced by both Christian and Hindu mysticism, Sufism has been both condemned and idealized in the Islamic community. There is considerable emotion in these practices which invite divine utterances, or poetry from the heart, and wild, whirling dance while in a state of divine ecstasy. Most famous of the Sufis was the poet Rumi, also the originator of the semi-monastic movement of dancers referred to as dervishes.

Tantra: A practice, originating in Hinduism, that requires surrender to the Goddess, or divine energy of creation. Two fundamental tantric paths have developed, a right-handed path and a left-handed path. The left-handed path is perilous and depends upon practices that are ritually impure and socially forbidden. The right-handed path depends upon extreme purification and rituals that promote strict spiritual discipline. Tantra is also the most prominent practice in Tibetan Buddhism, the origin of tantra itself attributed to the Buddha as a secret transmission. The path is essentially that of uniting the male and female principles of existence, which can be referred to as Shiva/Shakti.

Tao Te Ching: A work attributed to Lao Tzu, a legendary sage of ancient China, his wisdom written down and handed over to the guard at a mountain pass just before he vanished forever into the mountains. The philosophy of the *Tao* has two aspects, the Tao (or way), which concerns meditation and Te (or virtue) which concerns action. The Tao is described as both original being and the womb which has nourished the world. Virtue is born in us when we are in harmony with our ancient beginnings, the Tao itself.

Theosophy: The imagined meeting point of theology and philosophy. An occult movement, founded in the middle of the nineteenth century that contains elements of Buddhism, Hinduism, and, to a lesser extent, Christianity. Followers believe in reincarnation and subsequently the appearance of World Teachers who appear in order to teach the indestructible path of spirituality to the masses.

Upanishads: The *Upanishads* comprise a portion of the canon of Hindu scripture. They are scriptures that were composed after the Vedas, but unlike the Vedas are not concerned with achieving magical power but spiritual transcendence. They were begun by forest hermits and the term itself translates "to sit down at the feet of" (to receive a secret teaching). To this date the *Upanishads* remain a mystical teaching, rooted within orthodox Hinduism but with a message transcending all religious form and ritual.

Vedanta: A term for meditative practice and speculation based upon the Hindu *Upanishads*. The *Upanishads* "stand at the end of the Vedas," or the ritual practices that were the earlier form of Hinduism. The heart of Vedanta is *Avaita-Vedanta*, which projects that there is a nondual, pure being that is endlessly manifesting what we normally see as world—a philosophy thereby viewing the world as both the manifestation of pure being and an illusion hiding its true nature.

Zen: The extension of a Buddhist tradition, *Ch'an*, originating in China. Zen Buddhism considers itself a "special transmission" outside the teaching of all schools of traditional Buddhism. It refers to a mind-to-mind transmission of an ungraspable and undefinable enlightenment that, according to legend, began with a discourse of Buddha on Vulture Peak Mountain. Here, in order to expound an inexpressible doctrine, the Buddha held up a single flower and as a result of his gesture a single disciple became enlightened; Kashyapa smiled in response. Zen seeks to point to that Suchness which is not hindered by names or concepts, but is primordially pure and already perfect. Zazen, or sitting meditation, is not then a form of practice, but a realization of an innate perfection that not only predates all Buddhas, but is ever arising in the present.

ABOUT THE AUTHOR

Robert Boldman began experiencing the sublime energies referred to in tantra as kundalini as a five-year-old child. At nineteen, he experienced the apex of this practice that the Saint of India, Ramakrishna, described as Nirvikalpa Samadhi. At this early age, he found that he could rouse the kundalini in a receptive person and began teaching and initiating in tantra.

Eventually he grew disenchanted with "acquiring of experience and hoarding energy" and practiced for almost two decades in the traditions of Buddhism, meditating on emptiness. He gradually was "drenched in emptiness until it penetrated all normal experience." Practicing Zen, he became adept at haiku and wood block printing; his haiku has been published throughout Japan, Europe, and the Americas. Finally he practiced only mindfulness, renouncing all that he had accomplished. It was then that he encountered a retired priest who roused him from his torpor, encouraging him just to love, binding all that he had found with love.

Robert has since practiced as the priest encouraged him, finding that "both the emptiness and the light are included within love's matrix." He found that when, like love, he refused to be defined, he could then find rest "within the sheer radiance that is God's grace."

Robert studied Fine Arts and once sustained himself selling his paintings and drawings. He has since worked for thirty years in hospitals functioning as a paramedic, emergency room technician, registered respiratory therapist, and sleep technician. Most of his hospital experience has been in the realm of pediatric critical care.

He lives in Ohio with his wife of seven years, Loree.

HEARTSFIRE BOOKS

The evolving mission of Heartsfire Books is to celebrate spiritual evolution in the contemporary world with a series of books that inspire growth and promote physical and spiritual healing. We are privileged to present original and compelling writers who speak from their hearts and guide us to the magic of everyday experience.

Heartsfire Books publishes the *Heartsfire Spirituality Series*, including books on *Men's Spirituality*, and the *Heartsfire Healing Series*. If you have a manuscript that you feel is suitable for us, we would love to hear from you. Send a letter of inquiry with four chapters to: *Acquisitions Editor*, **Heartsfire Books**, 500 N. Guadalupe Street, Suite G-465, Santa Fe, NM 87501 USA.

Heartsfire Spirituality Series

Message from the Sparrows:
Engaging Consciousness
by Taylor Morris

The Emerald Covenant:
Spiritual Rites of Passage
by Michael E. Morgan

Inescapable Journey:
A Spiritual Adventure
by Claude Saks

The Alchemy of Love:
A Pilgrimage of Sacred Discovery
by Robert Boldman

Men's Spirituality

Gifts From Spirit:
A Skeptic's Path
by Dennis Augustine

Strong Brew:
One Man's Prelude to Change
by Claude Saks

The Search for David:
A Cosmic Journey of Love
by George Schwimmer

Heartsfire Healing Series

Healing Depression:
A Guide to Making Intelligent Choices
about Treating Depression
by Catherine Carrigan